Organis

Your Finances

A GUIDE TO GOOD PRACTICE

Organising Your Finances

A GUIDE TO GOOD PRACTICE

MAGGI SIKKING

AN NCVO PRACTICAL GUIDE

Published by
BEDFORD SQUARE PRESS of the
National Council for Voluntary Organisations
26 Bedford Square, London WC1B 3HU

ISBN 0 7199 1176 1

First published 1987

Typeset by D.P. Media Limited, Hitchin, Hertfordshire

Printed and bound in England by
Henry Ling Ltd at the
Dorset Press, Dorchester, Dorset

The National Council for Voluntary Organisations provides professional advisory services to voluntary organisations, protects their interests and promotes new forms of social action.

Other titles in the NCVO Practical Guides series:

Employing People in Voluntary Organisations
Finding and Running Premises
Government Grants: a guide for voluntary organisations
Starting a Voluntary Group: the legal choices
Voluntary Organisations and the Media
Voluntary Organisations and New Technology

Contents

Introduction

This book is about basic techniques of financial good practice for voluntary organisations and other small groups. It aims to help people who have day-to-day responsibilities for simple accounting tasks, for example, petty cash administration or paying routine bills. It also aims to help people who have responsibilities for financial planning, budgeting and record-keeping. All too often, voluntary organisations and other small groups have to call in expensive professional 'trouble-shooters' to sort out a mess that could easily have been avoided if a few simple guidelines had been followed. For, while voluntary organisations and small groups cannot get by without the help of a trained accountancy professional at certain times of the financial year, there is a lot that groups can do to help themselves, and to make the task of the professional more straightforward and, probably, less expensive.

'Accounting' often sounds difficult, mysterious, and perhaps a little frightening. But, in essence, accounting is no more and no less than simply measuring and recording an organisation's financial activities. That is to say, showing and proving where money has come from and where it has gone to. Book-keeping and accounting are ways in which we can describe how money moves through our lives and organisations. There is nothing prohibitively difficult about them.

In order to help you organise your finances, this book will tell you *how* to carry out some simple accounting tasks. But it is also concerned with explaining *why* they should be done. Understanding *why* accounting is important to any organisation is possibly the most important aspect of organising your group's finances. Once the *whys* of accounting are understood, then the *hows* of accounting will be far easier to manage.

This book will also help you to read and understand professionally-prepared accounts, and will suggest ways of using the information they contain to help you take long-term and short-term decisions affecting the future of your organisation.

Above all, the purpose of the book is to help voluntary organisations and other groups avoid that awful moment when, in panic, the accountant is called in, only to find that, nine times out of ten, it is already 'too late'.

Acknowledgements

I could never have undertaken this book without the help of friends and associates listed below who were prepared to edit, support, add to, criticise or expose their own mistakes for the general improvement of the text. I offer them my heartfelt thanks and appreciation.

Barbara Davidson, Julian Hodgson, Maggie Jones, Fiona MacDonald, Hugh Macpherson, Sue Mellis, Andreas Michaelides, Dick Millett, John O'Sullivan, Clive Palmer, Don Ratcliffe, Denny Wehner, Maureen Watson.

I should like to remember Pat Fitzgerald and Tom McAllister, and I must especially thank Andrew Cape who encouraged me in my early faltering steps towards understanding accounts. I would also like to thank the members of Gillygate Wholefood Bakery Ltd., upon whom he turned me loose for many years, and with whom I gained in confidence and knowledge.

1
Why Keep Accounts?

The most commonly given reason for keeping accounts is that it is a legal requirement. If a group is registered as a charity or a community co-op limited by guarantee, under company or co-operative law it is required by law to keep accounts and to have an annual audit. Additionally, a group may need to provide other people outside the organisation with a comprehensible record of its financial activities. Groups that receive funding or sponsorship are almost always accountable for how money is spent. This accountability becomes even more pressing where a group hopes to receive further funding in order to continue its activities.

Less commonly stated, but far more important, is the fact that good accounting practice does more than merely help you apply for grants or save your group from prosecution. It makes a group or organisation much more powerful and effective, and far more likely to achieve its goals. It maximises the value of the very commodity for which you have been standing in a cold market place selling raffle tickets or organising coffee mornings or whatever; that is, it maximises the value of your group's hard-won cash. It does this by giving the group information without which sound decisions cannot be made.

A still less commonly-stated reason, and perhaps a surprising one, is that good accounting practice builds confidence. It teaches people who are familiar with it a language and a way of working that are common to all groups, institutions and organisations, whether they are in the private or public sector or in the newly emerging 'third sector' which incorporates worker co-operatives and community co-operatives. Not only are people who understand it able to transfer their skills to activities outside the group in which they acquired them, and thereby enhance their own prospects, but it also equips them with useful tools for argument and questioning, as well as with useful information, when it comes to dealing with local authorities, charities, trusts, government, health authorities and so on. This type of confidence is becoming increasingly important as money for voluntary groups becomes more hard to come by.

What makes us think we cannot keep accounts?

Probably the greatest enemy of good accounting practice in voluntary organisations is the belief that managing money is extremely difficult and complicated, or, still worse, that money is in itself somehow corrupting or beneath notice. It is true that accountants *do* offer extremely varied and complicated services to groups who manage money, and frequently these services remain incomprehensible to those outside the accountancy profession. Added to this mystique about financial matters is the fact that many of us carry forward from our schooling a fear and loathing of sums which makes us believe we are incapable of adding up correctly, never mind 'keeping the books'.

Those of us who work in voluntary organisations are often very painfully aware of the need for money, either for our organisation, or for those we aim to support through our organisation. More often than not we work very hard to acquire it, whether through jumble sales at one extreme, or through major fundraising projects with commercial companies at the other. Yet when it comes to budgeting with money or making it central to our future planning we often throw up our hands in horror. It is not uncommon to find people working within voluntary organisations who think these are considerations for the business sector and not for charities or voluntary organisations at all. They feel that concentrating on money in itself debases their charitable aims and non-commercial objectives, that money is dirty and tarnishes their work. We need to understand how much better all of our efforts are served if we keep track of exactly how the money comes in and how the money goes out. And yet, even if we understand that good accounting practice will aid that effort enormously, we are still defeated by the belief that we are not capable or intelligent enough to really do it. In this way, it can be our attitude just as much as our lack of skills which lets us down.

Gaining confidence

One of the main purposes of this book is, therefore, to help people gain confidence in handling money. Confidence can be built in two ways: by trying and succeeding and/or by failing and understanding why. But it is also boosted by seeing that basic accounting skills are something practised all the time by almost all adults in everyday life. Whether you receive money as an unemployed person from Social Security, or as a director of a multinational company, whether you spend money on bus fares or on a new car, you find that money flows in and money flows out, and it often seems to flow out at an alarmingly rapid rate. Anyone who has money pass through his or her fingers knows that unless money is kept track of, expenses budgeted for, and income balanced against expenditure, they are going to be faced with an unpleasant shock sooner or later.

Confidence is also gained through observing that each voluntary group is not alone, either in trying to improve their accounting skills or in making mistakes. The experiences of groups of all sizes and from all over Britain are quoted throughout this book and give a voice to many accounting problems and successes common to voluntary organisations.

Moreover, it is not only voluntary groups who experience difficulties. Many businesses of all sizes struggle to make sense of their accounting practices and are just as likely as voluntary groups to go to their accountant with a carrier bag full of undated, faded till receipts. This is not a desirable state of affairs for any group, commercial or voluntary, but the knowledge that you are not alone can be useful when you work to overcome your financial organisation problems.

2
The Action Plan

This chapter is about writing an Action Plan for a voluntary group. This is similar to the sort of plan that small businesses often refer to as a Business Plan. It is a relatively unconventional idea for a voluntary group to consider writing an Action Plan and yet it can be enormously useful.

What is an Action Plan?

An Action Plan is a written document outlining the aims and objectives of the group. It lists the members of the group by name and identifies their individual contribution to the group. It describes where the group has its physical base and what material goods or facilities it owns or controls. There is an outline of the finance – where that money is expected to come from and where it is expected to go. Ideally the financial plan will be for three years so that both the group and those funding the group can have an idea of the targets that are being aimed for. Finally the group may choose to describe any future projects that it hopes to embark upon, or outline ways in which its direction may change.

The major effect of an Action Plan is that it concentrates the attention of all of those who are working within and for the organisation on exactly what its aims and objectives are, and on how they are expected to be realised. Of course, aims and objectives can change over time, but in most cases one would expect that they would remain largely the same. If they did alter radically, this might cause the original group to dissolve and a new one to emerge in its place. However, the methods chosen to achieve these aims might well change; indeed, it would probably be disappointing if they did not. For example, it is easy to image that the methods of fund-raising chosen in the first year of a group's work could change greatly as its work expanded. Jumble sales and coffee mornings might no longer be regarded by the group as an effective means of financing its objectives. Instead, the group could decide to appeal for funds from local businesses or to national grant-making bodies. Where fund-raising methods change in a way which is well thought out, the group should be able to re-evaluate its financial position effectively and so achieve its aims more readily. Without an Action Plan, it is arguable whether any voluntary group can accurately and quickly foresee that its chosen methods of financing its activities, whatever they may be, are in fact doing what it hopes they will do.

When faced with financial difficulties, a voluntary group may collapse for a variety of reasons. Morale may slump and members' attendance and interest may drop off. Or the group may dissolve because, after a year's hard work fund-raising, it may turn out that the most money was not in fact spent on supporting worthwhile projects. Instead a large proportion may have gone on paying travel costs for volunteers. There need be nothing necessarily sinister or crooked in this. It may be an honest mistake caused by bad planning, but it is doubtful whether after a year of such mistakes the group or its supporters would want to or feel confident to continue. An Action Plan might have saved it from this unhappy end.

The group may collapse because it is no longer certain what its aims and objectives are. Its members may have come together, for example, to provide 'information and assistance to the parents of Down's syndrome children'. Yet after a year the precise form that this information and assistance should take is in dispute. This need not be because group members are in any way selfish or argumentative, but it may well be because they are confused. There was no agreed written Action Plan as to how the group's general aim should be carried out.

A group may collapse because it fails to take advantage of the skills which exist among its members. The skills-profile of members which any Action Plan should include can often be very revealing. It is surprising how many people have capabilities which they demonstrate in the course of their daily lives and which they themselves fail to recognise as having any value. This is particularly true where people have not been in conventional employment for a long time. Profiles are often an easy way to identify skills in management. Beware of the 'I'm only a housewife/househusband' profile; running a house requires a wide range of management skills and self-discipline, which can be very useful to a group. Profiles can also be an interesting pointer toward identifying members' accounting skills. For example, pensioners living on a fixed income often have long and careful experience of budgeting.

The writers of the Action Plan may choose to write down only the barest bones of general detail, and the most elementary financial plans and forecasts, but they will and still have a useful working tool. The Action Plan may simply say:

Our group has been started to raise £5000 to fund an irrigation project in Tanzania.

We have three members. Wahida Begum is a local government officer, Daniel Adekola is a social worker, Finella Worthington is a housewife.

We need to raise £5000 this year in order to fund this project. Extra to that we also need to find £500 to cover the costs incurred in the course of the fund-raising itself. We expect to raise this money by sponsored walks, one in spring and one in summer; by inviting a well-known television personality to play a tournament of tennis for which we sell tickets sufficient to cover her costs and earn £1000 on top; by asking our local Lions Club to raise £1000; and by an auction of donated antiques.

While this plan is indeed adequate it does leave the reader wondering how they arrived at an expenses figure of £500. Guesswork? Experience? A commitment not to spend more than that and if more is spent to stand the losses personally? A more detailed plan would answer these questions and be more useful for reference in future.

Many voluntary organisations have their aims and objectives stated quite clearly in their constitution. What is important about the Action Plan is that it sets out the way in which these aims are expected to be achieved. An Action Plan can also be developed to give a very detailed forecast of expected income and expenditure. The following pages show an example of an Action Plan. Techniques for helping you decide what questions to ask when formulating your Action Plan are looked at more fully in chapter 6.

It is important to stress here that an Action Plan does not have to be as completely cut and dried as this example. As it happened, the reality of Chance For a Change's first year was quite different from its Action Plan. The group was unable to raise all of the required money from the activities it had planned and it had to run several extra jumble sales in order to reach its target. Additionally, its basic aims and objectives had to be reviewed as the members were unable to find anyone local to replace Ali when he had to leave at the beginning of the second year.

This experience does not invalidate the Action Plan. Firstly, the plan had generated the ideas that the group has used to design its activities for the first year. Secondly, when ideas are written down, it is far easier to monitor changes in them and then evaluate their impact to see whether the essential qualities of the original project remain. In this case, the group was faced with a short-fall, and was able to cope with it and make intelligent decisions as to how to go about coping. The group's financial records showed that jumble sales gave the best return for the amount of effort expended. So its members chose jumble sales to raise funds to recoup the short-fall.

Chance For a Change also needed to re-evaluate its stated aim that the project should employ a facilitator who was local to the area. The group discovered that this was no longer possible at the end of the first year. Did the members wail and tear their hair saying 'the group is unable to go on'? Not a bit of it. They returned to their Action Plan, they saw that this was only one of many stated aims and that amending it for the time being did not make the other aims impossible to achieve. They made the amendment in the knowledge that their original ideal

CHANCE FOR A CHANGE

A Hill Town Farm
Up North
Whereitrains
ENGLAND

History:

Chance for a Change was founded by Jo Friend in 1982 after she returned from a trip which included a visit to Nepal. While Jo was there she became friends with Ali, a local man, who was trained in agriculture and had worked with several of the major aid agencies stationed there. Jo and Ali shared a concern about the amount of money raised by large organisations that went to fund the administration of their operations. They were also concerned about the inappropriate scale of many projects, such as building expensive and under-used facilities like schools and roads in villages where people were ill and undernourished because of poor sanitation and crop failure.

Jo felt sure that she knew enough people in the UK who would be prepared to contribute on a regular basis to a project, provided that the project was small, was personally overseen by her and Ali, and entailed the minimum overheads for maximum effect. Jo and Ali calculated that the amount of money needed to fund simple technological developments which would improve the living conditions of the people of one village in the up-country would be £5,000 per year. (Their original costings are shown opposite.) Jo returned to the UK determined to raise this from friends and associates.

Aims and objectives

- Chance For a Change aims to raise an annual figure approaching £5,000 for the development of a village in Nepal. The development is geared to simple technological improvements in village life.
- The projects chosen are to be agreed by local people themselves as being appropriate to their hopes for their village.
- The projects chosen should be self-perpetuating wherever possible. That is to say, whatever is chosen should ideally be the sort of project which only requires an initial sum of money. It should aim to function eventually without outside funding by generating its own income.
- The key facilitator in the activities in the village should come from the village, or at least from the area.
- Skills must be taught to local people wherever possible so they can practise them when a facilitator is no longer available.

Members

- Jo Friend is a researcher who has travelled widely in her work for film and television.
- Jassu Anne Lilems works part-time as an editor of food information publications. She runs a small-holding and has sympathy with, and an understanding of, the problems which face small growers as well as a strong commitment to food issues world-wide.
- Ernie Lilems is a television director with experience of working with voluntary groups.
- Farrah Long is a dress designer for young people and works as a volunteer in youth and community centres.
- Louis Hepton is a free-lance journalist with a special interest in economics.

Budget

Forecast Expenditure 1985		
Wages for Ali (local worker)	£1,500	
Latrines 100 @ £1.00	100	
School Fees	200	
Training for barefoot midwife	200	
Dispensary stock	200	
Model vegetable patch seeds	200	
Start-up poultry stock	500	
Ali's expenses, i.e. stamps, stationery, travel etc	200	
Printing costs UK brochures, publicity etc	400	
TOTAL	£3,500	£3,500

Forecast Income 1985		
Returns from publicity shots	£1,000	
Annual bar-b-q	400	
Jumble sales and charity stalls	500	
Annual punks band and ball	600	
Covenants	1,000	
TOTAL	£3,500	£3,500

remained on the record and they could return to it once circumstances improved.

The Action Plan offers a voluntary group an opportunity for planning and control because it sets down clearly and simply how goals can be achieved. It also presents opportunities for criticism and change. Chance For a Change looked at its forecasts and noticed that it was expecting to spend £400 on publicity to generate only £1000 of income. With that information the members were in a position to ask 'is it worth it?'

Whatever detail is included in the Action Plan, whether it is a short version as in the first example, or a more detailed version as in the second example, the plan will at least represent the organisation more accurately than the unspoken assumptions and vague understandings which prevail in many small groups and voluntary organisations.

A well-written Action Plan need not take hours of time or great expense to be useful. Even in its briefest form it can be a document which forms the linchpin of an effective group. Apart from its usefulness as a guide in planning, and as an early indication of when things are changing or going wrong, it is an excellent, and after many years often very amusing, record of the group's activities, achievements and failings. The original workers will enjoy looking back to see how they have learned and where pitfalls and mistakes may loom again. Additionally, people new to the organisation can also see their current hopes and plans in the context of the group's history.

It may seem that the relevance of the Action Plan to accounting for voluntary organisations is limited. On the contrary, the first step in planning for finance is to agree and describe where you are going and how you are going to get there. This is true for businesses, whatever their size, and it is just as true of voluntary organisations. Money is a tool without which neither businesses nor voluntary groups can work. The ways in which they obtain it and the uses to which they put it is usually different, but both must account for it in their planning and in the records of their performance.

3

Straightforward Ins and Outs

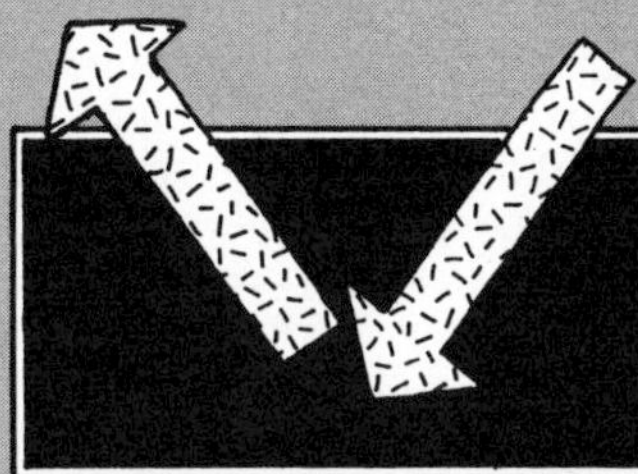

Keep everything is the first part of the golden rule of good accounting practice. This means keep every till receipt, every bill ever issued to your group, every letter or instruction from any official body. And when bills and receipts are not issued to you when financial transactions take place, ASK FOR THEM. Commonly you may hear 'you don't need a receipt if you write a cheque'. Untrue. You do. Ask again.

The second part of the golden rule is to ensure that when any transaction takes place the details of it are **accurately recorded**. This means filling in all the relevant information on cheque stubs, it means noting on till receipts from the supermarket checkout just exactly what the bill is for, and it means marking down in the paying-in book where this money has come from and when it is deposited in the bank.

The final part of the golden rule, and the part most often forgotten or never emphasised, is, having kept every offered scrap of paper, and having insisted on being given still more, **to keep those bits of paper in order**. An accountant who often works with voluntary organisations relates:

I used to have this sinking feeling when a client rang up from a local voluntary group and said, 'Adele, I'm bringing the books round this afternoon'. I knew these would consist of pristine ledgers with no entries, and a box full of incomplete and hard-to-read receipts.

In time I persuaded the group that every scrap of paper needed to be saved. Now I still have a sinking feeling when my client rings up. When she says that she is bringing the books round it still means pristine empty ledger books, which isn't too bad, but it also means several boxes and at least seven plastic carrier bags jammed and overflowing with every piece of paper which has come into her office during the year, from till receipts to bank statements, from shopping lists on the back of coffee-ringed envelopes which are supposed to justify cash expenditures, to their duplicated petty-cash vouchers, all jumbled up and squashed into a plastic bag.

The point is, of course, by all means keep everything, but keep it in a way that will make those items accessible and useful to your group. If you have no clear method of document storage in your group, or if you are just starting a voluntary group, then this chapter is for you.

Ordering and storing documents

First, open a bank account. A bank account means receiving regular bank statements and you should ask for them to be sent monthly no matter how infrequently you use cheques. These statements are in themselves a complete record of transactions through the bank. If you use the bank as much as possible for cash in and cash out, then a lot of the time needed to keep records can be saved. The bank statements will do the work for you.

Secondly, draw up a shopping list as follows:

1. 10 wallet files (in a variety of colours to help you grab the right one first time) *or* invest more money in a self-contained metal file box which contains 10 files.
2. a small stapler
3. a duplicate invoice book
4. some paperclips
5. some loose leaf ruled ledger/accounts paper with one wide column on the left hand side and 10 – 20 small columns marching across the paper from left to right.
6. a pack of cheap brown envelopes
7. a container for petty cash. A secure cash box is a good idea, but if the expense is too great an ordinary tin will do. Ideally whatever container you choose needs to be large enough to hold both the cash and also the accompanying paperwork such as till receipts, petty cash vouchers and so on.
8. a pad of petty cash vouchers
9. a ring binder
10. a hole punch

Begin by labelling the files, BANK STATEMENTS, BILLS TO BE PAID, BANK BOOK, BILLS WE

ISSUE, PETTY CASH, ACCOUNTS AND REGISTRATION, MISCELLANEOUS. Label the ring binder PAID BILLS. These files form a series of building blocks with which you can construct a simple accounting system. Throughout this chapter, and in chapters 4 and 7, each 'building block' is referred to in SMALL CAPITALS, so that you can more clearly recognise it, and how it relates to other building blocks as their uses are described. Keep the remaining files in hand for other uses as they arise.

Bank statements

Simply put them in the wallet in the order in which you receive them. You need them for the 'bank reconciliation' which should be done each month. You need them for the accountant at the end of the year. You need them to help you gauge your prospective income and expenditure.

Bills to be paid (purchase invoices)

When the bills come in for the 'phone, the rent, the electricity and so on write on them the day they arrived and file them. If there are many bills coming in all the time, then the file needs to be looked at each week. Nominate a day every week when bills will be paid. Go through the file and sort out those which need attention. Pay them. Return the file to its place until the same day the following week.

You need to be wary of paying both invoices and statements. An invoice records an amount owing for something at the time that thing has been supplied. A statement summarises the goods supplied within a given time period and may refer to several invoices. If you pay an invoice and then later pay a statement you may find that some things are being paid for twice. There are three ways to consider overcoming this problem. One is to never pay against a statement and to file them separately. In a separate file they will provide a complete year's record of trading with any one firm. Another is to throw all statements away the minute they arrive and continue to pay against invoices. A third method is to only pay against a statement and only then when you have found all of the invoices to which the statement relates and pinned them all to the statement itself.

If you feel that the number of incoming bills warrants a more sophisticated system then it is a good idea to file BILLS TO BE PAID in a file which has sub-divisions in it. Each divider needs to say when the bills within it are due for payment, for example, WEEK ENDING APRIL 26TH, WEEK ENDING APRIL 19TH, WEEK ENDING APRIL 12TH etc. These dividers can quite simply be sheets of scrap card or paper which stand out from the bills because they are a different size or colour from the bills in the file.

This way, when bills arrive which need to be paid immediately, and when bills arrive which do not need to be paid for three months, they can be sorted when they are received into their relevant 'due for payment weeks' and can be paid at the end of each week without the entire file needing to be sorted through each time. (There are still more sophisticated ways of handling incoming bills through the use of a ledger system. This will be looked at in chapter 4.)

BILLS TO BE PAID need to be kept in an orderly manner to avoid embarassing moments, like the events this group describes:

A local printer kindly agreed to print some information sheets for us at a much reduced rate and offered us three months credit. By the time three months had elapsed the donations we received could have paid the bill a hundred times over. So we had the cash. But we had, in the excitement of such a good response, quite simply forgotten to pay the bill. It was with great embarassment on both sides that we were reminded that it was outstanding. We still feel very badly about it and are uncertain whether we can approach the printer for help in the future.

Bills also need to be kept in an orderly manner so you can at any time have a good idea of how much money you owe altogether. This is vital for evaluating on a regular basis whether you are meeting your financial targets. It is all very well to feel happy because you have a total of £200 coming in in one week from donations if there are few or no bills to be paid in the file. But if you find that there are £200 worth of unpaid bills it puts rather a different complexion on your financial circumstances!

Paid bills

The easiest way to keep bills well ordered is to pay them by cheque. Quite simply write the cheque number which was used to pay the bill in the top right hand corner. File them in numerical order with the most recently paid bills on the top. Keep these in a ring binder. Over a year quite a few bills may accumulate and the ring binder will be the only way to keep them in the exact order in which they are filed.

Paying by cheque and filing bills in a ring binder means that you can almost instantly find any bill that you have paid by cross referencing from the BANK STATEMENT file or from the BANK BOOK. If someone rings up and says 'where is my money?' you should be able to answer very quickly if it has been paid by cheque.

Additionally, paid bills are a comprehensive record of what you have bought. It also means that if, for example, you are ordering tea, coffee, milk and sugar from one supplier then that bill will tell you what was spent on each item. This is essential information for preparing costings for the future and for monitoring price increases.

Where bills are paid by cash they are accounted for as part of petty cash and are recorded in the PETTY CASH file.

Petty cash

This can be a nightmare, usually because many more people in an organisation will have access to PETTY CASH than to the other areas of the group's finances. Therefore there are plenty of opportunities for discrepancies to occur in the record of ins and outs.

As a consequence the PETTY CASH file needs to be kept up-to-date regularly. Not only will regular up-dating pick up errors right away, but if errors are found quickly it is far easier to jog someone's memory about a problem which can only have occurred during the preceding week than to ask them about a sum of money which was spent well over two months previously. This recollection from a voluntary organisation is a chastening one:

We operated a petty cash system where everyone took out their bus fares, postage and so on and just wrote it down. When the cash got low we drew another £50 from the bank. This went on for about a year. By the end we discovered we had drawn over £1,000 from the bank but could only account for £600 of it.

All that needs to be done for a PETTY CASH system to work well is to use what is known as the Imprest System. This means you need to record diligently what goes out onto petty cash vouchers (*see* figure 1a) and to check them each time you need to top up PETTY CASH. So, if there was £20 in the tin at the beginning of the week and there is now only 12p left, there should be receipts stapled to vouchers to the total value of £19.88.

It is important to record on the vouchers/receipts what the amount was for. Often these receipts will simply be supermarket till receipts, either faint because the machine producing them was barely inked, or tattered and worn because one of your members has been carrying them around in a pocket for days. Is the receipt for milk or postage or bus fares? Each of these will come under a different heading in the final writing up of the PETTY CASH book.

Once the receipts and vouchers have been found and the amounts balance, draw a cheque for £19.88 which will then 'top up' the amount in the PETTY CASH to the original £20. Clip all the receipts together, stuff them in a cheap brown envelope. Seal it, number the envelope with the cheque number that was used to draw that amount, punch holes in the side of the sealed envelope and file it in order in the PAID BILLS file.

Very occasionally, someone will want £50 in cash for a single payment. If you are operating a PETTY CASH system based on a maximum amount of £20, as in the above example, a cash payment of £50 can throw a group into panic. First you should question

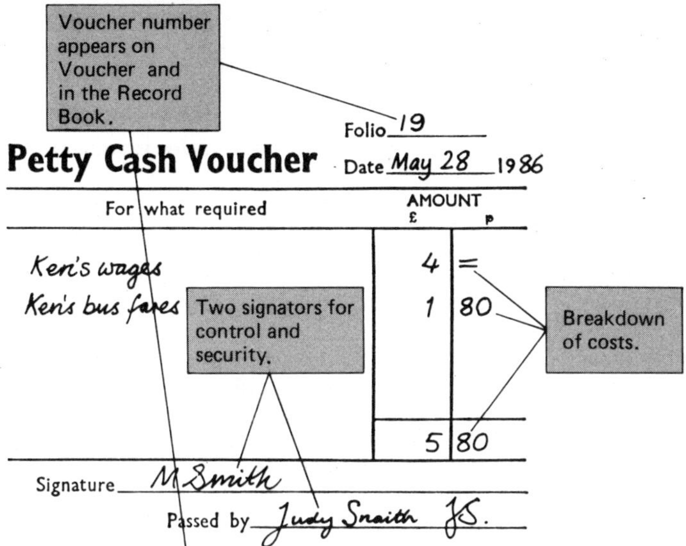

Fig 1a

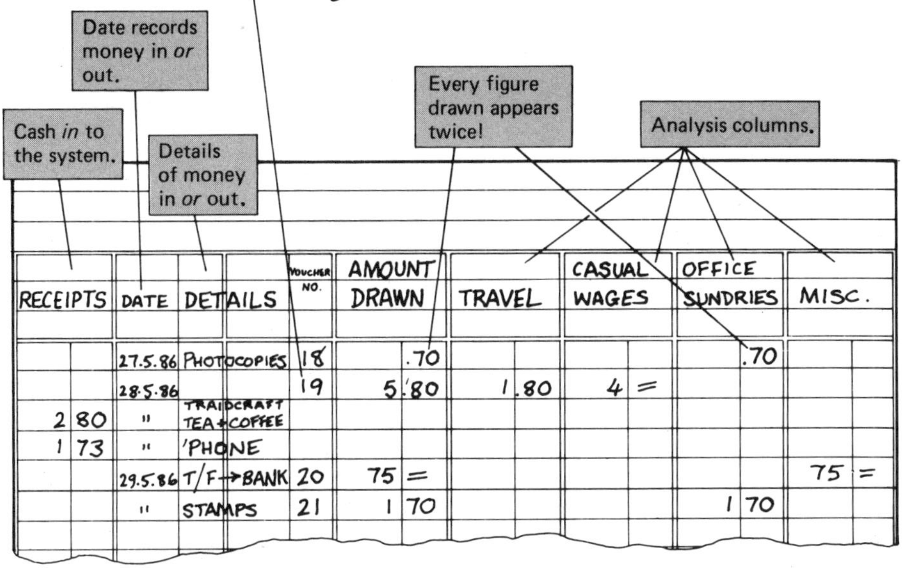

RECEIPTS	DATE	DETAILS	VOUCHER NO.	AMOUNT DRAWN	TRAVEL	CASUAL WAGES	OFFICE SUNDRIES	MISC.
	27.5.86	PHOTOCOPIES	18	.70			.70	
	28.5.86		19	5.80	1.80	4 =		
2 80	"	TRAIDCRAFT TEA + COFFEE						
1 73	"	'PHONE						
	29.5.86	T/F → BANK	20	75 =				75 =
	"	STAMPS	21	1 70			1 70	

1. Balance the Petty Cash book by adding the figures in the Amount Drawn column. This should equal the transport, casual wages, sundries and misc. columns added together. Subtract the money recorded as shown from the receipts. This should equal the actual cash in hand.
2. Note that the surplus cash was transfered to the bank on 29.5.86.

Fig 1b

whether indeed a cash payment of £50 is really called for. It is irregular to pay out such a large cash amount and you may wish to encourage the payee to accept a cheque.

If you find you really do need to pay out £50 cash then quite simply go to the bank and draw the full cash amount, in this case £50, and file the relevant document (i.e. whatever it is that justifies the payee's claim for cash) in the PAID BILLS file with the cheque number at the top, as you have done for all of the others. In fact what you are doing is paying a cheque against an invoice as you would in paying any normal bill, but instead of giving the payee a cheque you are taking an extra step by going with that cheque to the bank and drawing it in cash for the payee. Paid in this way, the £50 has nothing to do with your PETTY CASH system at all.

The record sheets shown in figure 1b are the sheets upon which the vouchers need to be recorded. You will see in the figure that the analysis columns are the means by which you can know in a year how much was spent on casual wages, how much on postage, how much on volunteers' travel and so on. These sheets record the activity of the PETTY CASH over a year in a concise way and both your group and your accountant can know at a glance what sort of financial activity the PETTY CASH covers over any period.

The PETTY CASH is the main area in all organisations, voluntary and otherwise, where money can go missing and records can become out of control. The Imprest System is good insurance against this happening. If there are discrepancies then these will come to light frequently and can be dealt with, hopefully by jogging people's memories, or, if necessary by writing the amount off as 'missing'. Where large amounts are missing then there are clear indications that something more serious may be wrong, and the information is there in your records to support any remedial action you decide to take.

Where a PETTY CASH system is troublesome to operate it may well be that some sort of managerial changes are necessary. In chapter 8 managerial difficulties are examined and some ways of dealing with the access and control problems of PETTY CASH are suggested.

Bills we issue (sales invoices)

What is true for the BILLS TO BE PAID is also true for the BILLS WE ISSUE file. Keeping track of them means you can ring up after the agreed credit time has elapsed and ask quite legitimately 'where is our money?'

BILLS WE ISSUE are equally important to a financial picture as the BILLS TO BE PAID. If £200 worth of BILLS TO BE PAID are balanced by £200 worth of invoices for which you still have to receive payment then you *can* relax!

Bank book

This is usually a book, but these are very expensive, and if you make mistakes can quickly become very untidy. Loose leaf sheets work just as well and need to be kept in this file. The BANK BOOK is sometimes known as the CASH BOOK and is very simply a record of what goes through the bank. All cheques that you write are recorded in the BANK BOOK. Anything paid into the account is also recorded in the BANK BOOK. It is an extended version of the BANK STATEMENT. It fills in the detail that the BANK STATEMENT leaves out, such as the name of the person to whom the cheque is made out, and what the cheque was for – tea, seeds, travel, wages and so on. Figure 2a gives a sample lay-out of such a page.

The BANK BOOK is also always more up-to-date and accurate than the bank statement. A BANK STATEMENT will only tell you the state of the account on the day that the statement comes out. Since cheques always take a minimum of 3 days to clear you may well have written hundreds of pounds worth of cheques that do not show up on the bank statement and so the statement will give a far rosier picture of your financial situation than is in fact true.

Without the BANK BOOK you cannot reconcile what your cheque book records with what the bank records on its BANK STATEMENT. This exercise is shown in figure 2b. It

JANUARY 1986

DATE	BANK	DONATIONS	PUBLIC SPEAKING	V.A.T.	OTHER
7.1	29 30	29 30			
"	16 30		16 30		
21.1	300 =				GRANT 300 =
	345 60	29 30	16 30	— —	300 =

RECONCILIATION

INCOME	345 60	BANK STATEMENT	(311 95)
LESS EXPEND.	(981 21)		
	(635 61)	LESS ANY UNPRESENTED CHEQUES	(38 =)
ADD LAST MONTH'S BALANCE	285 66		
	(349 95) ✓		(349 95) ✓

Fig 2b

DATE	NAME	CH. NO. (070)	BANK	V.A.T.	OFFICE SUNDRIES	PLANT & EQUIPMENT	TRANSPORT	REPAIRS & RENEWALS	FUEL & PHONE	VOLUNTEERS' EXPENSES	MISC.
1.1.86	J. MUNROE	182	25 =							25 =	
"	T. GREENWOOD	183	20 =							20 =	
"	J. GRANT	184	10 =							10 =	
2.1.86	P. JUDGE	185	25 =							25 =	
11.1.86	COLYER LTD.	186	41 =	2 67	20 50	17 83					
"	M. WARREN	187	33.87							33 87	
"	MAC GARAGES	188	10. =				10 =				
14.1.86	RUDD INS. BROK.	189	45. =				45 =				
"	J. WILD	190	670. =			670 =					
"	J. WILD	191	20. =			20 =					
24.1.86	PETROL	192	5. =	.65			4 35				
"	BRITISH RAIL	193	32. =				32 =				
"	M. WALLACE	194	6.34							6 34	
"	B. DAVIDSON	195	38. =						38 =		
			981.21	3 32	20 50	707 83	91 35	— —	38 =	120 21	— —

Fig 2a

is vital that the writing up of the BANK BOOK is done from your cheque stubs and not simply by copying the bank statement. If you do not write up the BANK BOOK this way then the reconciliation with the BANK STATEMENT will be a worthless activity. You cannot be sure that what the bank has recorded as the activity on your account for the month agrees with your own understanding of what has happened. This is because if you simply copy from the statement then you are not really comparing what the bank has recorded with what you have recorded in your own system.

Reconciling the BANK STATEMENT with the BANK BOOK will tell you if people have cashed the cheques that you wrote for them. So if you receive a reminder threatening you with your gas being cut off when you know you have issued a cheque, you will be able to tell by reconciling the BANK STATEMENT with the BANK BOOK whether in fact the cheque has cleared. Likewise, if you have a yearly standing order for a publication which you have forgotten about, then doing a bank reconciliation will remind you. The same is true of other standing orders or direct debits relating perhaps to rents or insurances.

Banks sometimes make rather dubious charges for services rendered and reconciling the BANK STATEMENT regularly is a good way of keeping an eye on any of these. Apart from charges on overdrafts and perhaps loan agreements, they also sometimes make charges for their staff's time if a group goes to discuss a particular problem with them. While this is rather rare in the case of a voluntary organisation, it has been known to happen and is worth looking out for.

Finally, the BANK BOOK transfers from the often grubby and battered cheque stubs the details of every payment and arranges them neatly and clearly so that almost everything needed to be known about any payment can be seen at a glance. Of course the cheque number is also there, and this corresponds to the numbers written on the PAID BILLS, thereby completing a useful cross-reference. Additionally, when the columns themselves are all added independently they not only act as a balance check on the bank column as is shown in figure 2b, but they also let you know for every month how much was spent on what. This makes compiling a monthly picture of what your organisation has been doing a great deal easier and more accurate than simply going through your cheque book.

Accounts and registration
This is a file for keeping all the past year-end accounts of the organisation, along with the records of the group's registration, be it a community co-op, a registered charity in its own right or one of many groups under an umbrella organisation. It is surprising how many times one can be asked for sight of any of these documents or for copies of them. The accounts especially will be useful to the group in helping it form decisions for the future, and in making grant applications.

Miscellaneous
This file should house any important correspondence, such as items concerning rate increases, new insurance information, covenants and so on. Wherever correspondence is of a continuing nature, as in a dispute, for example, then there is a case for opening a file for that correspondence in its own right. But often throughout the accounting year there are items which need to be kept which relate to the financial health of the group and for which there is no real need to open a separate file.

The activities surrounding these all files are for the most part very important to the effective running of the group. Certainly life is made easier for the accountant who will no longer have a 'sinking feeling' nor need to face sorting through stuffed carrier bags, but, most importantly, life is also made easier for the group itself.

This chapter has looked at the more straightforward ins and outs of organising finances. With a little effort, keeping these files and their care should easily become routine. Nonetheless there can still be difficulties to overcome. The first is how to remember to do all the jobs. Many people who help to run voluntary organisations or other small groups are involved on a very part-time basis, so this is an important consideration. It can be great help to have regular monthly meetings at which finance is discussed along with other general issues and problems. This will mean that whoever is in charge of the record-keeping will know that there is a date every month by which he or she must have some figures prepared for the group to discuss and act upon.

Even if an agreed accounting procedure is adopted, preparing monthly financial information can still be a burdensome task for a single member of staff or volunteer. One solution could be to arrange one day or evening a month when everyone involved with the finances and book-keeping will agree to meet, do the work and then go for a drink or a meal as some sort of reward for work well done.

A different kind of problem may arise when the person responsible for the accounting tasks is efficient and good at their task, enjoys the work, and yet is thwarted by others who forget to ask for receipts, or, having asked for them, promptly lose them. One voluntary group relates how they tried to cope with this:

Mick never asked for receipts. In the end we said we could no longer refund him money for purchases without having a receipt. The first few times he did have to go back and ask for one, but in the end he remembered.

It is important to remember that many small voluntary groups are staffed by people who put in a great deal of effort out of the goodness of their hearts, but, unfortunately, that the goodness of their hearts does not always mean that they do things the 'right way' in accountancy terms. Nonetheless, while a group is small, doing things precisely the 'right way' is not so desperately important so long as they are done in a way that can be deciphered and understood. Provided that the information is there and has been recorded in an orderly manner, then a professional accountant can write a formal set of books if necessary. But, whatever your formal accountancy needs, the major aim of good financial record-keeping should be to help you to understand your group's finances, and to help you use that financial information to the best advantage of your group and those you aim to support.

Moreover, once you have set up and run a very simple and cheap system, such as the one outlined in this chapter, it will be much easier to implement any new, more formal ways of doing things if your accountant asks you to try them the following year. You should, in any event, always feel free to ask your accountant how your record-keeping might be improved so that any final, professional, accounts can be easier, and therefore cheaper, to produce. Your accountant's answers will probably make more sense once you have tried a simple system for a year, since then you will actually know why and how an accounting system works.

4
More Complicated Ins and Outs

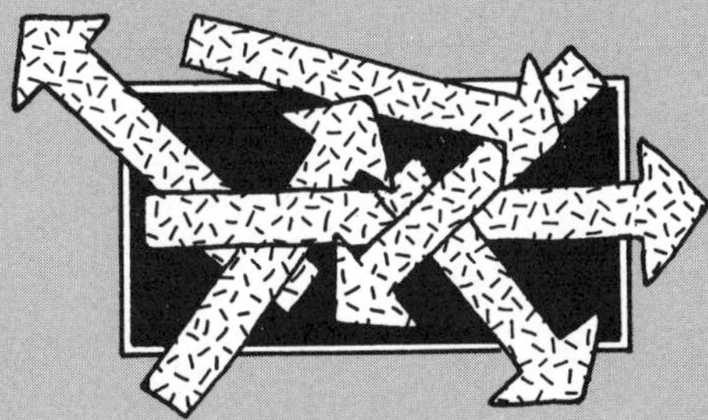

This chapter is about more complicated accounting procedures than those described in chapter 3. Many of these are quite sophisticated and will not be necessary for small organisations. Most of them will require refinement for your group's use. But it is worth reading through this chapter to see whether your group could benefit from changing from the simpler techniques outlined in chapter 3 to some accounting methods which are more complex and more comprehensive.

There is a limit to how much you can expect to learn about in-depth accounting systems from a book. There is definitely a point in the pursuit of accounting knowledge where you should stop and ask advice from a professional, or at least from someone with greater experience than yourself. It may well be that once you start considering complex changes to your accounting methods this point has been reached. Even if you decide to ask for advice from an accountant, there is still a case for using this chapter to refresh your memory about certain methods after the accountant has left you to get on with a new system. Equally, it may help to remind you about the benefits which may result from using them.

Multiple Systems

Multiple Bank Accounts

If you receive grant funding from several different bodies, and if you are accountable to each of them, operating several bank accounts can be helpful. The following describes a good example of multiple funding:

- *We receive a grant from the local authority for our day-to-day running costs, a grant from MENCAP for work relating to people with mental handicap in particular, and a small grant from the local Townswomen's Guild towards soft toy manufacture.*
- *The local authority wants to see how much we have spent on office expenses, how much on travelling expenses, how much on wages.*
- *MENCAP wants to see how much has been spent on developing training and skill identification for people with mental handicap, how much has been used in identifying work places for these people, how much has been used in creating work places and so on.*
- *The National Federation of Townswomen's Guilds wants to see how much money has been spent on fur fabric, on thread, on new sewing machine needles, on kapok stuffing.*

In short, each grant-giving body wants to know how the money they have given to the group has been spent. Often this will be so that they can be sure that the money has been used responsibly and for the purpose for which it was given. Local Authorities and large charities have very strict guidelines under which they must operate, and so they will naturally be vigilant about the smaller groups which they support. They need to check, so do not resent their questioning.

With smaller-scale, locally-based funding, where monitoring may be less stringent, the funding bodies may instead want to make sure that the money they have donated is doing some good. This is important because it helps them to maintain their morale and also the momentum of their own fund-raising efforts. If, as in the above example, there is a local grant toward the cost of soft toy-making, it is helpful for the grant-giving body to be able to tell their own members, for example, that 600 soft toys were made at the cost of £300 which were all sold at £3 each and thus the mentally handicapped workers had been able to raise £1,500 toward the purchase of their mini-bus. This sort of information helps the grant givers not only to *feel* that their efforts have been worthwhile, but it also helps them to *see* quite clearly that their donations have been put to good use.

In the above example three bank accounts could be operated. One for the local authority funding, one for the MENCAP monies, and one for the grant from the

Townswomen's Guild. A simple system, as described in chapter 3, could be operated for the most part on all three accounts. BANK STATEMENTS, INVOICES and BANK BOOK will all need to be kept for each account and a BANK RECONCILIATION performed on each account monthly.

Slight complications will occur when a bill arrives, for example, the 'phone bill, where there is no breakdown of costs under three headings. Clearly it is easy to see that kapok stuffing is a cost that should be paid from the Townswomen's Guild money, but in the case of the 'phone bill, where *all* the activities of the voluntary organisation have contributed to it, the total amount needs to be divided between all three accounts. To find out which calls were made and received on behalf of which area of the groups activities could be done, but it would probably require a full-time paid worker to monitor, and would be a silly waste of resources.

So a group in this situation can agree a breakdown for the phone bill based on a rough estimate. In the above case, probably at least 70% of the calls made and received would be costed against the local authority income which was given to the group specifically to cover day-to-day running costs. If the group made a large number of phone calls to help young people with mental handicap look for employment, then 20% of the bill could be allocated to the MENCAP account. The remaining 10% would be costed against the funding for the soft toy-making.

The payment of the invoice would then be dealt with as follows. Divide the bill up as per the agreed proportions and write a cheque on each account for that amount. Send them off. On the bill itself write the breakdown and the accounts from which each figure has been paid. Photocopy the bill twice. You will now have three bills, the original and two copies.

On the top right hand corner of the original write the cheque number of the cheque which paid the greatest amount. File it, in this case in the PAID BILLS file which relates to the local authority account. On the next copy of the bill write the cheque number in the top right hand corner of the cheque drawn on the MENCAP grant account. File this bill in the PAID BILLS file which relates to the MENCAP account. Finally on the remaining copy write the cheque number in the top right hand corner of the cheque drawn on the Townswomen's Guild account and file it in the PAID BILLS file which relates to this account. Whenever you undertake this sort of procedure be sure to file the original copies of the bills in the PAID BILLS file where all the other original bills are kept. In the above cases, the local authority PAID BILLS file is suggested, as the local authority grant contributed the largest share of the group's income. Ensuring that all original bills are kept together means that when an original is required of any bill, either by you, or by the accountant at the year end, there is no question as to which file holds it.

If your group does not have ready access to a photocopier, or if photocopying is too costly, then simply file the original in the PAID BILLS file which you have decided is to be the file where all the original bills are to be kept. For the other two accounts, file a sheet of paper showing the amounts paid, any VAT or other sub-total figures, mark the relevant cheque number in the top right hand corner and then make a note of where the original bill if filed. For example, write 'see original, PAID BILLS file L.A. (local authority) Account. Cheque no. 456235'.

In some ways you may feel that running three accounts triples the accounting work load. Untrue. Certainly there are three sets of books and reconciliations to do, but the existence of three accounts simplifies the monitoring of what money is for what. If you need an overall picture, this can be based on combining BANK STATEMENTS, which also form a complete record of transactions against which you can check your own records. Bank statements are recognised by everyone as being an accurate account of the activity of an organisation and therefore most groups to which you may be accountable will be satisfied with the correctness of this procedure.

Of course, keeping the BANK STATEMENTS alone will not be enough. The analysis of the figures which go through the PETTY CASH system will also be important to the organisation and to the grant-givers. It will be vital to ensure that the analysis of these transactions is recorded for each account just as described in chapter 3 under BANK BOOK and as shown in figures 2a and 2b.

Deposit Accounts

So far, only current accounts have been considered. There may well be times when a group will want to deposit large sums in a deposit or investment account. There is a very simple way of coping with the records concerning monies in accounts other than current accounts. Deposit *all* monies in the current account in the first instance. Then transfer them from the current account into the relevant deposit or investment account and transfer the amounts back as required. The current account and the BANK BOOK then automatically still record all the financial transactions of the group, and the current and deposit account can, for accounting purposes, be considered as one account.

If you receive large sums of money all at once, designed to fund your project for a year, there are several things to bear in mind. There may be a good case for looking at how that money might earn some extra funds for the group. Voluntary groups with charity or co-op status often consider a deposit account with their bank. You need to ask the bank to deposit your money in a 'gross interest-bearing deposit account' so that your interest is not taxed at source and you receive the full benefit to which you are entitled. You will probably need to show the bank manager your registration documents before this can be agreed. You can also look at depositing money with the Charities Deposit Fund, details of which are given on page 63.

Choosing to deposit funds in order to earn interest may, on the face of it, seem a good idea. The following groups have interesting comments on this practice:

Our group is involved in famine relief. In our second year we received a large grant to carry out our work for the next six months. We looked at investing the money in a deposit account but then abandoned the idea. To us it seemed ridiculous that we should be working to alleviate famine on the one hand, and then, in our view, giving the large banks our cash to use to perpetuate famine on the other.

We are a small group working with mentally-handicapped young people in youth clubs and in sheltered workspace throughout the city. Although we are only a small group with a very limited brief, we do see ourselves as connected with all voluntary action everywhere, be it development work in the Third World or down and outs in the inner city. We will not invest our money. We accept that our decision may seem insignificant or even 'cutting off our noses to spite our faces' but we simply do not feel that we should use a system of money generation that is dubious, to say the least, to further our goals.

Our group is involved with development education. We have often had disagreements about the investment of our grant monies, and we expect the discussion to continually re-occur. But, so far, we continue to invest to maximise the value of our cash. We explain it in this way: the economy of voluntary action the world over is a weak one, we need to get as much money into that economy as we can. No one is helped if we abandon that responsibility in the mistaken belief that we are somehow better, or cleaner, for not having invested funds for the best reward.

Multiple Petty Cash Systems

Wherever you operate multiple accounts the question of a multiple petty cash system must also arise. It will no longer be possible to operate the straight-forward petty cash system outlined in chapter 3. You may feel you need to ask advice, but essentially the choices you have are either to operate three completely separate systems along the lines of the single system in chapter 3, or to continue a single system with a more complicated means of recording and analysing the amounts.

In either case there will be pitfalls if your management of petty cash is weak, a topic discussed more fully in chapter 8. The three-system approach does tempt 'borrowing' between systems, which can result in a hopeless muddle. One group remembers:

We thought we were being very clever instituting a multiple petty cash system. As you might expect they each needed topping up on different days. The seemingly endless trips to the bank encouraged us to borrow from one box of petty cash in order to top up another box. That was fine while it was infrequent and while we remembered to note down IOUs. But in time we were less vigilant and as a result the system finally broke down altogether.

Noting down the different accounts against which petty cash is to be drawn can also be tiresome. If you choose to operate a single system and yet you need to keep petty cash records for different sections of your income, it may be helpful to have different coloured petty cash vouchers, or, if those are unavailable, to take different coloured felt-tip pens and run them down the sides of the voucher pads so that you can use a different colour for each account.

Day Books and Ledgers

The recording system outlined in chapter 3 is, in effect, a simple ledger system. It is perfectly adequate for sorting and keeping various vital pieces of paper in the right place. Changing from that method or something very similar is in most cases quite unnecessary. Explaining how to keep day books and ledgers is beyond the scope of this guide. What this section can offer is brief discussion as to why you might need these systems and how, in general, they work. If your group is large enough to require day books and ledgers then it is important to go to your accountant for their advice.

Day books and ledgers in themselves are just bound volumes of ruled paper. They are set out to help you provide a detailed record of the financial state of an organisation at any time. The layout is such that you can quickly analyse the figures and summarise them so that any aspect of your group's activities is identifiable at a glance at best, and at worst after an hour or so of extracting figures from the ledgers.

Creditor and Debtor Ledgers (also known as *Purchase Ledgers and Sales Ledgers* or *Suppliers and Customers Accounts)*

These ledgers are part of the book-keeping systems of most commercial firms and often do not seem relevant to voluntary organisations or small groups. However more and more voluntary groups are actually 'earning' their income by providing a product or service for sale. Trades clubs or community centres are long-established examples of such groups where tea, coffee, alcoholic beverages and meals are served for a profit which in turn is used to support the centre or club's activities. Sometimes a group may need to set up a separate trading organisation in order to retain their charitable status, with the main charity acting as a type of holding company, receiving profits and owning plant and equipment. The legal structures available, and the implications of any choices, need to be fully discussed with a professional advisor before taking any steps. Some books which discuss the options available are listed on page 62.

Let us look at a community centre with a catering facility as an example of one type of organisation where creditor and debtor ledgers might be used. Obviously, regular purchases of foodstuffs and beverages will be necessary in order for the centre to provide catering. The goods for sale may be bought on account, which means they are not paid for until some time after they have been used. Purchases on account should be recorded in the Creditor Ledger. This will show exactly how much money is owed by the group to suppliers at any particular moment.

Then imagine that this catering group, apart from providing meals within the community centre, is also offering outside catering to local organisations, for which it makes a charge. And imagine also that it bakes several dozen scones daily, which are supplied to the Meals on Wheels services. Now we can see that this community centre is also offering goods and services for which it is not immediately paid. These amounts must be accounted for by delivery notes and invoices issued to the clients who are 'buying' the service, which in this case, is outside catering, or scones. These amounts should be entered in the Debtor Ledger. At a glance, this ledger will tell us just how much the group is owed.

The hope is that there will never be consistently more debtors than creditors, that is to say, you always hope to be owed more than you owe others. If that is not the case, then these ledgers will enable you to discover the discrepancy before it is too late. They should form a key component of a good credit control system whereby a member of the organisation with responsibility for monitoring credit to customers can easily identify bad payers who need chasing.

There is no cast-iron way to avoid losing money because people will not or cannot pay. These unfortunate instances known as bad debts should be rare and will be taken into consideration at the end of the financial year when the accountant will either carry them forward into the next year or else 'write them off', which means formally recognising them as a loss to the organisation. Nonetheless, there is a great deal that groups can do to ensure that bad debts are rare. One precaution is to have a clear and written policy as to how to decide who shall receive credit and how much that credit should be. Another is to have a set of procedures for chasing payment. People will often pay those creditors who make the most fuss first, so letters and reminders can be a way of speeding up payment.

Whether or not you choose to operate systems of ledgers like these, the key thing to remember is that once a voluntary organisation is involved in trading, then in financial terms, it has to get organised, just like any other trader. It will need to make commercial decisions, and to run a commercial system of book-keeping, and to do both in an efficient and professional way. Making decisions and good accounting go hand in hand, and the financial planning and monitoring systems that you choose need to be well thought-out and suitable to your organisation's requirements.

Sales Day Book or *Outward Invoices Book*
In chapter 3 a simple method for filing invoices was described. Where your organisation issues many invoices for a wide range of products or services you will need to consider a Sales Day Book or Outward Invoices book which will form one of your set of ledgers. Just as with the other ledgers for your group you will need to seek good professional advice as to how to proceed.

Issuing invoices is an important part of record-keeping and whenever you supply something that is to be paid for after the goods or service has been received, you must have a written record of it. No matter how good *your* memory may be, the payment into your group of monies owed by others must not be dependent on any one person's memory.

Moreover, it is important to exercise some judgement as to when it is appropriate to offer credit at all. Whenever you offer to let people pay for something after they have received it you are offering them credit, and you have to record somehow that the money is owed to you. This is usually done by issuing an invoice stating the amount owed. Issuing an invoice means time and money – the time taken to write the invoice out and the cost of the paper on which it is written. Writing out reminders for unpaid invoices costs time and money in exactly the same way as the original invoice, plus a postage stamp and an envelope. Make sure you know how to get hold of anyone who is going to owe you money. If you are unable to find an address then the cost is more time and perhaps no money – if you cannot find out where to send your reminder then it is quite likely you will never be paid.

Voluntary organisations are often staffed by people who do paid work, or volunteer, out of a sense of commitment to a 'good cause'. It is important to remember that not everyone you do business with will act from similarly high principles. It may be true that those who use your group's services are good-hearted but merely forgetful. It may be that they are neither good-hearted nor forgetful but have just happily taken advantage of your photocopying service or your stationery or your computer time or your tea and coffee with no intention of honouring your invoice. In addition to deciding on a policy on credit sales, it is also important to decide whether the use of your services, such as photocopiers or computers, should be for members or affiliates only, whose names, addresses and support for your group are already on record, or whether you want to open your services to the public at large. It is also important to decide when invoices are a good idea and when payment should be requested immediately. Writing out invoices for less than £5 is usually wasteful of resources.

Purchase Day Book or Inward Invoices Book

A Purchase Day Book is a more formal method of cataloguing bills as they arrive than the two procedures suggested in chapter 3. On a daily basis, usually at the beginning of the day as the post arrives and is opened, the incoming bills for payment are listed in the Purchase Day Book. The date, the name of the supplier and the amount is all that it is necessary to record. These details can then be written into the Creditor Ledger pages and then finally paid and filed.

The Purchase Day Book is extremely valuable when an organisation has a great many bills coming in daily. It is possible to see on a day-to-day basis just how financially committed the group is, who has sent in their bills, and it ensures that none 'get lost'. Like all of the day books and ledgers discussed in this section, the Purchase Day Book forms a key part of a chain of book-keeping procedures. Diagrams of just how these ledger systems work together as a check and balance on each other and as an enclosed system of record-keeping and accounting are shown in figures 3a, 3b, and 3c. A checklist that your group might also find useful is shown in Figure 3d. The purpose of these diagrams is to put into pictures what this section has been describing and to offer those groups who are already operating a system of ledgers an opportunity to re-examine their methods.

Wages

Wages may be paid according to one of three systems:

P.A.Y.E. (Pay As You Earn)

Pay As You Earn is the standard wages system operated by all employers in Britain. If you are going to employ a worker who is not self-employed and who is not going to work with you on a casual basis, then you will need to register with the Inland Revenue and inform them that you wish to operate P.A.Y.E.

Paying as you earn means the employer subtracts the requisite National Insurance Contributions and income tax from the employee's total gross wage. It also means that the employer must pay the Employer's Contributions toward National Insurance while the employee is earning. An employee's total earnings are referred to as the *gross earnings* and the earnings after contributions have been paid are known as *net earnings*.

The Inland Revenue will provide you with everything you need to operate a P.A.Y.E. system (including a plastic wallet to keep it all in) with the single exception of the wages book in which to record it. The instructions and the forms that are currently given to employers are clear and well presented. If there are any difficulties do not hesitate to contact the P.A.Y.E. officers in your area. They are usually very glad to help.

The wages book for recording P.A.Y.E. is expensive and by no means worthwhile if you are employing fewer than 10 people and paying them monthly. You can easily rule your own paper for a record of the P.A.Y.E. and it will serve just as well. Figure 4 is an example of the headings you will need to include.

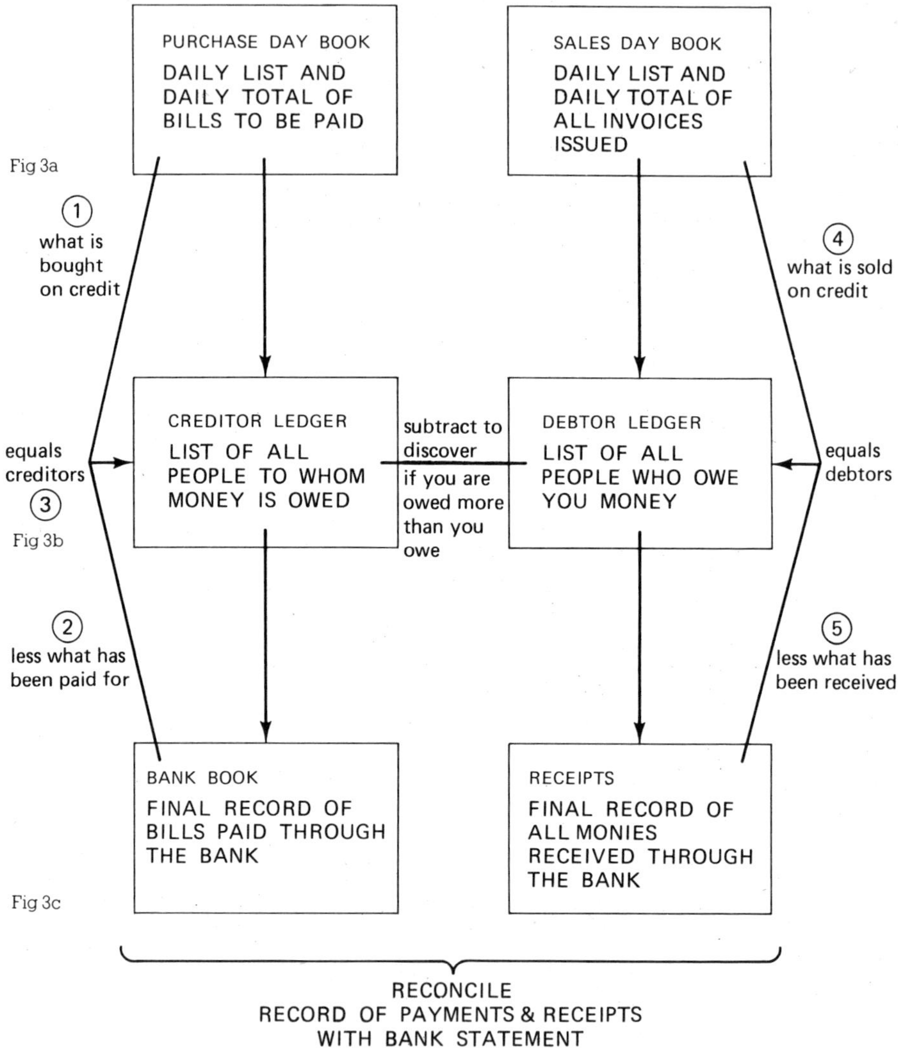

Fig 3a

Fig 3b

Fig 3c

CHECKLIST

1. Do you supply and are you supplied "on account" a great deal?
2. Do you handle large amounts of cash?
3. Are you in part a trading organisation?
4. Are many of your accounts on different time scales?

Fig 3d

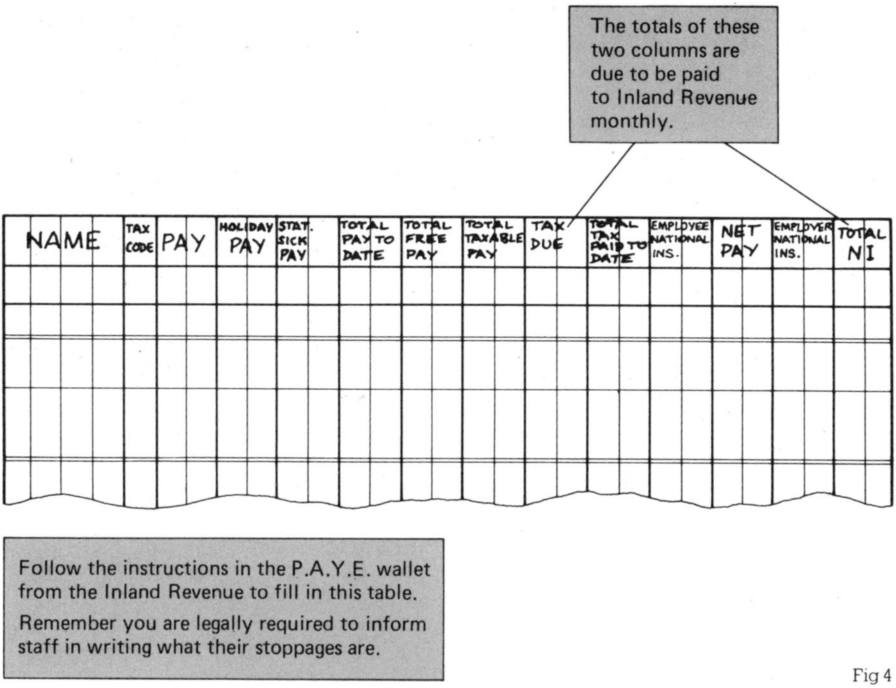

Fig 4

Self-employed workers

If someone is truly self-employed then you have no responsibility for them under the P.A.Y.E. system. They are responsible for their own National Insurance contributions, and for their own arrangements if they become ill or pregnant or whatever. They must provide your group with an invoice for their work and you should pay it in the same way as you would pay any other bill.

If someone who is self-employed works for you there may be insurance implications for your group which you will have to examine carefully. Certainly money will be saved by using people who are self-employed, because no employer's contributions to National Insurance will have to be made. But on the other hand, they will often need to charge more for their time and services and so the real savings may be doubtful. Finally, bear in mind this group's experience:

We elected to employ Christa three full days a week. She was already working as a book-keeper offering general office work from home and came highly recommended. As she was already self-employed we decided to pay her against a monthly invoice.

She began halfway through our financial year and did an excellent job. She was our only paid worker.

The trouble was that we never quite knew how to describe her. She wasn't employed by us and so it was always hard to identify just what her role was when both volunteers and the public came into our offices. She couldn't officially sign our VAT return or act for us with the accountant. Was she part of our organisation or wasn't she? Somehow that became a very important issue for us and eventually we had to resolve it.

Casual workers

These workers are individuals who would normally expect to be paid from the petty cash. They usually offer infrequent services to your organisation, and have either no regular hours or very few. The normal amount per week that an organisation would expect to pay a casual worker would in 1986/7 be no more than £37.99 per week, the current threshold for National Insurance contributions.

Anyone who is paid as a casual worker will need to have their name and address recorded in a casual workers book for the reference of both the accountant and the Inland Revenue. You will also need to confirm that you carry the sort of insurance appropriate to their employment.

Value Added Tax (VAT)

Value Added Tax can be described simply as a cheap way for the government to collect taxes. Certain products and services are called Standard Rated Goods and as such are liable to VAT: electrical goods, business consultancy, adults' clothing, food served in restaurants and hot food to take away are some familiar examples. Some goods are called 'zero-rated', which means that no VAT is currently charged on their sale. Some examples of zero-rated goods or services are foods bought in a supermarket or a shop, books, and postage.

Where a group or an individual is registered for VAT they must charge VAT on those products or services which they supply and which are Standard Rated Goods. In this way, VAT is in effect 'collected' by the group and is then passed on to the government when a VAT return is filed and paid. Similarly, the VAT paid on any VAT invoices which the group has paid can be claimed back.

When you complete a VAT return, which is usually done every quarter, you list the total VAT you have received. This is the VAT which you have charged your customer or client on any services or products you have provided. You also list the total VAT you have paid out on bills where you have been charged VAT. This includes both the VAT you have paid on bills that have been paid by cheque and on bills that have been paid through the petty cash. You subtract the VAT you have charged from the VAT you have paid and then pay Customs and Excise what you owe, or, if you have paid more than you have collected, ask them to send you any money they owe you.

Should we register for VAT?

In community food co-ops where food is bought in bulk and then broken down into smaller amounts for sale to members of the co-op at a small profit, it is often possible to pay out VAT for bags, sellotape, telephone bills etc while not needing to charge any on sales. In this case, it might seem to be in your interest to register for VAT and you may do this voluntarily even if your turnover is below the usual VAT level. But here you should proceed with caution. It is not unusual for groups to be ignorant of the fact that *grant income exists outside VAT. It is neither subject to VAT, nor can VAT be reclaimed on any purchases made with grant funds.* A group could easily register for VAT voluntarily and then end up paying out more VAT than it will get back. So before registering, consult an accountant and your local VAT office. VAT officers are usually very helpful and quick to answer any queries your may have.

For many people, there is no choice over registering. Every individual and every organisation with a turnover in 1986/87 of £20,500 or more is required by law to register for VAT. Turnover means the total amount of money coming into an organisation, excluding grant funding, within a given period of time. It does *not* mean profits. So the amount of money coming into a group does not need to be very large before registration is required. However, unless your grant income is very small and your income from some sort of trading and sales is very high, VAT registration is unlikely to be necessary for most small groups.

If your group is not registered for VAT, then there is no need to operate a VAT column in any of your records. (If you do need to record VAT, then the amount to write down is the total amount of VAT you have been charged on any bill.) Many groups are unclear about how to record

VAT, and it is not uncommon for accountants to receive books from groups who are not registered for VAT where the VAT has been extracted from the records completely, even though it has been paid, or where the total amount of any bill, often including VAT, has been entered in the books and then VAT added to that! To repeat; if in any way you remain unsure about how to proceed with VAT then it is important to seek advice from a professional or from your local VAT office.

Conclusion

The purpose of this chapter is simply to draw attention to the various choices and systems that can be used to undertake accounting jobs within your organisation. If your organisation is using all or some of the methods outlined, then reading through this chapter may have acted as a reminder of the purpose of keeping accounts and records in these ways. It should encourage a re-evaluation of your existing systems so that you can look carefully to see whether they are providing the information and guaranteeing the efficiency your organisation requires to operate effectively.

5
Budgets and Cash Flow

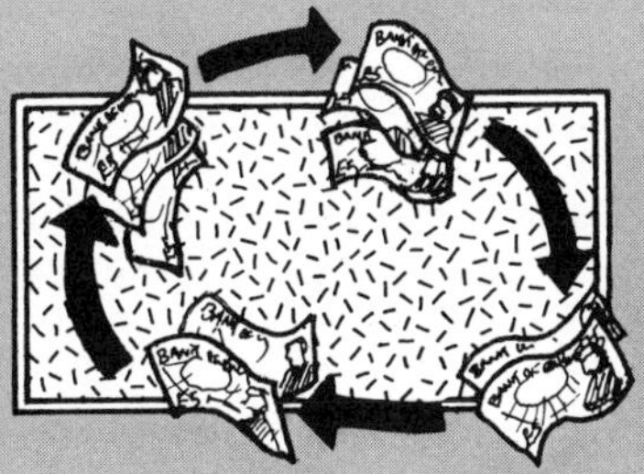

Learning from the past in order to predict what might happen in the future is not something which applies only to our personal lives. Nor are predictions to be looked for only on visits to fortune tellers! They are something that can be done by using an organisation's accounts. Learning from the past and forecasting the future, in accounting terms, are known as Budgeting and as Cash Flow Forecasting respectively.

Budgeting Costs

Budgeting is predicting on paper, to the best of your ability, what the costs you are going to incur are likely to be. In organisations these predictions are normally set out to cover an entire year's operations, broken down into months. Figure 5 suggests some headings that a typical organisation might use. Under each heading a figure is then predicted for the total spending in each month.

These predictions are usually arrived at by looking at what happened in preceding years. Thus, if a group spent a certain amount on heating and lighting their premises in one year then they will be very likely to spend the same sort of sum in future years. It also means that if the price of fuel has risen over the year then an extra sum will need to be allowed for. If you have taken on extra rooms, or extended your opening hours, or are running more equipment, then you will need to allow for that in the budget, too. Equally, if room or equipment use has diminished and prices have remained the same or decreased then the budgeted figure should reflect this.

There are questions you should ask yourself while preparing a budget which are a useful way of focusing your mind. The following list gives some general examples:

1. What are the amounts we expect to spend this year which will remain the same month by month?
2. When do yearly costs like the MOT of a vehicle occur?
3. When do quarterly bills, e.g. for the telephone, fall due for payment?
4. Are there any other payments which occur once every 2, 4 or 6 months?
5. What extraordinary costs are likely to arise, perhaps costs associated with moving premises, taking on new staff, buying a vehicle, typewriter, photocopier etc?
6. Are there work programmes that we are committed to and which need to be planned for in financial terms?
7. What are the hidden costs in paying any wages, like National Insurance contributions and pension contributions?

The evidence from preceding years is a very useful guide. But there are also things that you should be able to forecast accurately, not just estimate. You should know how many people, if any, will be employed by the group and what their exact wages over a year will be. You should know what any rates or rents on any properties will be, and if you do not know, you should find out by contacting the landlord or local authority and obtaining some sort of written confirmation from them as to what your costs are going to be.

Even if you cannot forecast accurately, budgeting can be almost like a guessing game and yet still be useful. This is particularly true of what is called 'Zero-based budgeting'. That is to say, budgeting that is not based on accurate information from the past. This budgeting will normally only be done once during the lifetime of an organisation; when it first begins to function and when there are no financial records to refer to when planning for the future.

There will be other times when an organisation may need to consider zero-based budgeting. One example would be when a group is going to undertake an entirely new project. The following group report describes just such a situation:

Our work was concerned with home-help, i.e. housework, for people with disabilities. But in the course of our work, we began to think there was a need for housebound people to have pets and our initial informal enquiries evoked a very positive response.

We decided to launch a formal program

		JULY	AUG	SEP	OCT	NOV	DEC	TOTAL
1	SALARIES	972 =	972 =	972 =	972 =	972 =	972 =	5832 =
2	SECRETARY SERVICES	25 =	25 =	250 =	25 =	25 =	25 =	375 =
3	RENT, RATES INSURANCES	53 =	53 =	178 =	53 =	53 =	53 =	443 =
4	FUEL & 'PHONE	100 =	100 =	100 =	130 =	140 =	160 =	730 =
5	OFFICE SUNDRIES	20 =	20 =	220 =	20 =	20 =	20 =	320 =
6	ADVERTS	10 =	10 =	10 =	– –	– –	10 =	40 =
7	TRANSPORT	50 =	50 =	50 =	50 =	50 =	50 =	300 =
8	PUBLICATIONS	17 =	17 =	17 =	17 =	97 =	17 =	182 =
9	MATERIALS	150 =	150 =	30 =	30 =	30 =	90 =	480 =
10	MISC. & PROF. FEES	– –	– –	400 =	– –	– –	– –	400 =
	TOTAL	1397 =	1397 =	2227 =	1297 =	1387 =	1397 =	9,102 =

Gaps left for ACTUAL figures.

This figure cross balances, down and across.

Notice how high the budgeted costs are for September. The end of the financial year is in August. In September there is the accountant to pay on line 10, the annual report & accounts to type up (line 2) on lots of paper (line 5) and post (line 5).

Note how fuel costs are expected to rise toward mid-winter.

An insurance premium falls due in September (line 3).

Fig 5

to find, settle and support suitable pets with suitable owners and homes. This was quite a departure from our original aims as a group although we all still feel that it is a part of our general aim to suport people who are disabled in some way.

We had to draw up two separate budgets, one for the home-help side and one for the pet placement side. Now, some of our support funding is given exclusively to one side or the other.

Once a small organisation has been functioning for some time zero-based budgeting along these lines is relatively rare. There is, however, one way in which zero-based budgeting can be used regularly as an exercise to help clarify your ideas. On the face of it, it may seem a silly idea to ignore past information when trying to predict the future. Yet it does have one considerable advantage: by paying no attention to what has happened before you can come to preparing the budget with a clear and fresh mind, often doing a better job from 'zero' than from sifting through evidence of last year's expenditure.

If you have to plan your budget from scratch your guesses need not be wild or uneducated. If, for example, your group was trying to estimate its telephone expenses, it is very unlikely that you would estimate more than £150 on telephone expenses during the group's first quarter. Why? Because £150 per quarter in 1986 would be a high telephone bill for a household, and most people involved in budgeting for their group will have experience of household telephone bills, or be able to ask people with telephones what their quarterly bills amount to. Of course, if your group makes most of their calls at peak rates then the estimates may need to be increased to take account of this. If, by referring to the average household telephone bill, the group decide that an estimate of more than £150 is appropriate, because they intended to use the telephone a great deal in the course of their activities, then that is fine. But the decision in either case has been based on some knowledge, research and experience, even if these do not relate directly to the group's activities.

It is relatively easy to allocate enough money for expenses with which you are familiar. Unknown costs are more difficult to estimate, and it is important to allow enough money for these in your budget. The only way to do this is to try to budget costs too high. This will often predict the worst picture. This is not such a bad thing. In a perfect world, of course, one would hope to predict the correct picture. But, in the absence of perfection, predicting expenses as greater than they turn out to be is infinitely better than predicting them to be less. There are three reasons for this:

Firstly, when you come to compare the budget with the actual figures as they become known month by month, you will see that there is more money available than you hoped. This generates a comfortable feeling of 'bonus' – rather like finding a ten pound note in your pocket which you had forgotten was there!

Secondly, it is a great boost to morale for a group to feel that they have been able to keep their own costs well within their estimates and thereby release more money for the work that they have come together to support.

Finally, even by predicting an inaccurate picture, a system of careful planning and monitoring can demonstrate to members of an organisation the various assumptions about their group's financial position that have been used to help formulate policy and plan expenditure. Most important of all, it can raise the question of precisely how the group expects to achieve its aims.

Budgeting Income

Obviously you will want your expenses to be covered by your income, otherwise you will be in trouble. Figure 6 shows a sample lay-out for income budgeting for a group which receives most of its money from a local authority grant. In trading organisations it may be far more difficult to predict income accurately. There, the success of

Gaps for the ACTUAL figures.

		JULY		AUG		SEP		OCT		NOV		DEC		TOTAL	
1	LOCAL AUTH. GRANT	1500	=	1500	=	1500	=	1500	=	1500	=	1500	=	9000	=
2	TRAID-CRAFT SALES	150	=	150	=	100	=	75	=	50	=	200	=	725	=
3	PUBLICA-TION SALES	50	=	50	=	50	=	50	=	50	=	100	=	350	=
4	PUBLIC SPEAKING FEES & EXP	–	–	–	–	100	=	100	=	100	=	–	–	300	=
5	PRIVATE DONATIONS	20	=	20	=	20	=	20	=	20	=	20	=	120	=
	TOTAL	1,720	=	1,720	=	1,770	=	1,745	=	1,720	=	1,820	=	10,495	=

This figure cross balances down and across.

Notice increased Traidcraft Sales as Christmas approaches. (line 2).

Public speaking is non-existent during summer months and picks up as the academic year begins (line 4).

Fig 6

reaching budgeted targets is dependent upon factors like marketing and the cost of transport in a far more direct way than for organisations which receive their funding through grants or fund-raising.

Trading and fund-raising are fundamentally different. Traders need to sell something that people *want* – that is why people buys things. Without a careful study of the market, a trading voluntary organisation, like the community centre in chapter 4, may bake scones for their cafe and in the end have to feed them all to the chickens because not a single member of the public comes in to buy them, or, having come in, chooses a chocolate bar instead. In contrast, many voluntary groups are *asking* for financial support. They hope the 'customer' will feel that the aims of the group are worthy, and that they will buy scones to help the cause even if they do not particularly want them. There are, of course, many occasions when the 'customer' of a voluntary organisation also gains something that they want from the transaction, but this is not always essential to the exchange.

The impact of the commercial market for non-trading voluntary organisations is not so immediate. Therefore the financial activities of this type of group need to be planned and predicted in a different way from those of small commercial firms. When you draw up a budget for income you may find that the headings under which you list your projected income are numerous and varied. This is because in most cases there will be some financial reward associated with almost any of your group's efforts. If you have a jumble sale there will be some income from it. If you schedule a coffee morning, there will be some income. If you hold a raffle, there will be a financial result, and so on. And if, for any reason, the income from one of these is below target then a group is free to think up new ways of attracting funds with very little, or no, capital outlay. This means that for only a very few pounds spent you can arrange a further coffee morning, another mail shot, one more press release to local radio to attract donations and so on. This is a different level of planning and expenditure from that required, for example, when launching a new range of imported knitwear, or setting up a shop or cafe.

A non-trading voluntary organisation or other small group will therefore need to have a flexible attitude toward the predictions it makes about the income that it generates. At any time it may need to re-evaluate its budget for the next month in the light of the preceding month. In an example given in chapter 2, on page 9, the group set out how it expected to generate its income. It had budgeted its income from four events; a sponsored walk, an appearance by a TV personality, an appeal to other local charities, and an antiques auction. If one of those events did not take place, or did not raise the amount hoped for, then the group would need to try to raise money in a different way later in the year, and that would need to be re-evaluated in the budget.

Where a group has few expenses, no 'phone and no wages, then these alterations to the budget will have few uncomfortable repercussions. But where a group has many outgoing commitments this sort of change can be quite difficult to adapt to. Budgeting and monthly accounting are very important indeed where groups carry month-to-month financial responsibilities.

Where a group's income comes entirely or mostly through grant funding there is often a tendency to believe that budgeting is irrelevant. A local authority-funded sheltered workshop made the following comments:

Because we were in receipt of money from the council to run the workshops we didn't bother to draw up budgets. We knew roughly when the bills were coming in, what we could hope to sell, and more or less how much the council had committed to us.

That was the trouble. The more or less of the situation! The council was paying us monthly. Fine. Except it was to be two months in arrears! Had we drawn up even a relatively slack budget, or at least commit-

Add the figure brought forward to the budgeted income.

Subtract the budgeted expenditure from the total forecast income.

	JULY	AUG	SEP	OCT	NOV	DEC
B/F	– –	323 =	646 =	189 =	637 =	970 =
TOTAL INCOME	1720 =	1720 =	1770 =	1745 =	1720 =	1820 =
	1720 =	2043 =	2416 =	1934 =	2357 =	2790 =
TOTAL EXPEND.	(1397 =)	(1397 =)	(2227 =)	(1297 =)	(1387 =)	(1397 =)
CASH FLOW.	323	646 =	189 =	637 =	970 =	1393 =

Carry this figure forward to the next month.
This is the forecasted "cash in hand" for the month.

Fig 7

ted something to paper, we might have avoided the traumas of not being able to pay bills, and even worse, of not being able to pay our own staff. We could have gone to the bank with our predictions and arranged an overdraft to cover the interim period.

A budget will draw a financial picture for you. You need that picture just as much if you have a fixed and secure income as you do if your income comes in in dribs and drabs from various fund-raising events. Budgeting is to help you avoid lean times, or at least to prepare you for them so that when they do come you will not be caught out.

Cash Flow Forecasting

Cash flow forecasting is really just a short way of saying, 'when the time comes, will we have enough money to deal with this situation?' Budgeting is concerned with predicting costs and income in any given time period. Cash flow forecasting takes that income and subtracts those costs to arrive at the actual amount available to an organisation to spend in hard cash at any time. Then it accumulates the totals as shown in figure 7. This accumulation is done so that you can clearly see that in some individual months, like September, the situation looks quite dire, but that during July and August the organisation receives a lot of money; the accumulated cash flow shows that the overall situation is quite healthy.

Cash flow forecasting is impossible to separate from budgeting because the forecast is based on the budget for money coming in and money going out. Without some prediction of what monies might be expected to come in and what might be expected to go out, cash flow forecasting cannot take place.

The example on page 38 of the local authority-funded workshop illustrates the importance of cash flow forecasting. That experience is common to many small commercial firms as well as to voluntary groups. They can have money owing to them (as the local authority owed the workshop money when it was paying two months in arrears), they can have orders on the books (the workshop had a job to be done and people who needed to be there in order to do it), and their future prospects can look bright. They just do not have any money NOW to pay their staff, or creditors, and neither their staff nor their creditors can or will wait two months. As a result the business folds or the workshops have to close.

In the case of the sheltered workshop, cash flow forecasting could easily have indicated potential problems. The management committee could have written to the council to ask them to pay more speedily, showing them in writing why this might be crucial. They could have approached the bank for an overdraft to cover this foreseeable eventuality. They could have delayed taking on a new member of staff. They could have delayed payment for another month for the oil for the heating system. They could have bought the oil in the summer when it was cheaper, and so on. The point is, had they been in possession of a cash-flow forecast then there were any number of arrangements that they could have made to avoid finding themselves in trouble financially.

Conclusion

A frequent response from groups when faced with the facts of budgeting is to say 'so what' or 'it's obvious'. They are often puzzled to find that there is not something very mysterious or clever about budgeting. It involves only the simple techniques described in this chapter. Even though a group with a wide range of activities handling a great deal of money may have quite a complex budget, the basic idea behind budgeting is very simple.

The fact that people find it simple, however, does have its dangers. Because the idea of budgeting is so simple, some groups think that it is not important to the effective running of their organisation, or else they believe that because it is simple then it can be quickly cobbled together at any time.

Budgeting and cash flow forecasting, important as they are for all groups, become even more important when a group is short of money or needs to set financial targets in order to boost morale. They can identify the amount of money required to continue the desired range of activities and can also help to spotlight any areas, if they exist, in which expenditure can be trimmed down.

Additionally, a month-by-month budget makes it possible to compare actual records of past income and expenditure so that the group has an up-to-the-minute picture of what is going on. This is an invaluable tool of financial management for informing a funding body of any unexpected changes in expenditure which may affect further applications for funds.

6
Official Accounts and the Audit

Imagine the following. The accounting year is over. Your records are immaculate or near immaculate. Off you trot to your accountant and hand in all the necessary documents for them to prepare the end of year accounts. The accountant is very prompt in preparing them and returns them to you typed up neatly, bound in a folder. The first page is the title page. The second page says the standard thing about the accountant being satisfied that the accounts have been prepared correctly and based upon accurate documentation. So far so good.

The next page shows the Income and Expenditure Account and the final page shows the Balance Sheet. Now the panic sets in. The following group's remarks about their end of year accounts are representative of the reactions of many small voluntary organisations and other groups when first faced with their accountant's final accounts:

The accounts looked great when they arrived. For a few moments we all felt quite proud of ourselves. Here was the record of all our financial achievements over the year in a professional presentation.

Then we turned over the first pages to look at the figures, knowing that our careful financial preparations would be represented here, and half expecting to recognise some of the very figures we had ourselves recorded.

Nothing had prepared us for our dismay and near panic when we first looked at those pages. We simply couldn't understand them at all! We felt dismay because we had worked so hard to keep good records for the accountant for the end of year accounts and we could not immediately see what use this had been. We felt panic because we couldn't think how we were going to explain the accounts to our supporters. The Balance Sheet was the worst of all. What was balanced with what?

The Final Accounts

In order to tackle some of these difficulties, which are expressed by many voluntary organisations in trying to understand their accounts, a set of model accounts is printed on the following eight pages. The format is the precise format that you are likely to encounter in any formal set of accounts. On each page there are boxed comments to help clarify small points. At the bottom of each page there is a box of general explanations relating to the page.

How you can change your accounts

All statements of final accounts will have certain things in common, a Balance Sheet for example, or an account of Income and Expenditure. These pages are drawn up by the accountant by referring to your group's own records, and they cannot be altered to project a different picture. Nonetheless, there are things that you can do to try to improve the picture that the accounts present.

Firstly, you can ensure that the presentation of the accounts is neat. This means that you can bind the pages together with an attractive cover. You need only look at the type of presentation that building societies and enterprise boards use to have an idea how dressed-up final accounts can eventually be.

Secondly, you can add a page outlining in greater detail the aims and objectives of your organisation, and give some examples of things that your group has achieved during the past year.

Thirdly, you can request your accountant to make available a Receipts and Payments account like the one in the model final accounts given in this chapter. A Receipts and Payments account, as you can see, is a record of what has been received and what has been paid out in one year only. The figures are arrived at by simply amalgamating all of the information in the CASH/BANK BOOK and the PETTY CASH BOOK into one set of figures. The Income and Expenditure Account shows two years of figures set out side by side, and is often a shortened version of the Receipts and Payments

CALDERDALE DEVELOPMENT EDUCATION GROUP LIMITED

(C.D.E.G. Limited)

ACCOUNTS

1986

CONTENTS

The status of the organisation, that is to say limited company, plc, charity, will depend on the constitution agreed by the original members.

Your accountant or local Council for Voluntary Service will advise you about charitable status for taxation purposes.

C.D.E.G. Limited

Report of the Management Committee

The Management Committee present their sixth Annual Report for the year ended March 31st 1986.

1. *Activities*
   The aims and activities of the Company during the year remained unchanged from previous years. They were to continue to heighten awareness of development issues through printing and distribution of leaflets and booklets and to offer courses and lectures throughout the authority in schools and institutions.

2. *The Management Committee*
   The members of the Committee during the year, some of whom are life members in accordance with clause 45 of the Articles of Association, were as follows:

   June Grant
   Farida Begum
   Rita Smith (joined May 1985)
   Freer Griffiths
   Phil Oxtoby (joined August 1985)
   Basharat Hussain
   Gordon Jones (resigned September 1985)
   Ann Lendal

3. *Company Status*
   The Company is limited by guarantee and all members have, therefore, agreed to contribute a sum not exceeding £1 in the event of the winding-up of the Company.

4. *Charitable Status*
   The Company has charitable status for taxation purposes.

5. *Auditors*
   In accordance with Section 14 of the Companies Act 1976, a resolution proposing the re-appointment of Adele Naseem A.C.A., Chartered Accountant of Bradford, to the Company will be put to the Annual General Meeting.

BY ORDER OF THE BOARD

June Grant
Secretary
May 1986

This simply refers to a rule in the constitution which requires you to appoint an auditor by a resolution of the company. The organisation's constitution will outline any and all of such requirements.

AUDITOR'S REPORT
to the Members of
C.D.E.G. Limited

We have examined the Accounts on pages 5 to 7 and have carried out audit work in accordance with Approved Auditing Standards.

In common with many organisations of similar size and organisation, the Company's system of control is dependent upon the close involvement of the employees who are also members. Where independent confirmation of the completeness of the accounting records has not been available, we have sought assurances from the members that all the Company's transactions have been recorded in the books and records.

Subject to the above, in our opinion the financial statements, which have been prepared under the historical cost convention give a true and fair view of the state of the Company's affairs at March 31st 1986 and of its deficit for the year then ended and comply with the Companies Acts 1948 to 1985.

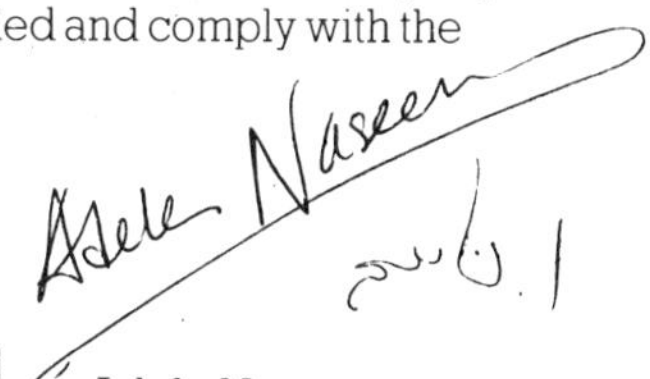

June 1986

The signature of the accountant must appear here.

Adele Nassem
Chartered Accountant
Bradford

Historical cost convention means that all the figures are stated at their original purchase value. No account is taken of inflation or an asset's current value.

C.D.E.G. Limited

ACCOUNTING POLICIES

DEPRECIATION has been provided at 25% per annum on the straight line basis on all classes of assets.

GRANTS are taken to income on a receivable rather than a received basis. Grants receivable in the current year comprise:

	1986	1985
	£	£
Voluntary Services Unit	28,000	32,945

TAXATION
C.D.E.L. is a registered charity and there is, therefore, no provision for taxation in the accounts.

Depreciation is simply accounting for the fact that capital items like cars and typewriters do eventually get 'used up' exactly as paper and stamps. It just takes longer. In these accounts these items are being used up over four years and one quarter of their value is being written off in each of the four years.

This allows for grant income which is confirmed as coming but which has not yet arrived.

C.D.E.G. Limited

RECEIPTS AND PAYMENTS ACCOUNT
for the year ended March 31, 1986

RECEIPTS:	£	£
Grants		28,000
Sundry other income and Fees		177
Bank Interest		963
		29,140
PAYMENTS – REVENUE		
Salaries	24,731	
Subcontracting Services	352	
Secretarial Assistance	823	
Rent, Rates and Insurances	997	
Fuel and 'Phone	1,337	
Postage, Stationery, Adverts	1,537	
Materials	157	
Subscriptions, Publications	384	
Transport	2,066	
Sundries	351	
Bank Charges	39	
Audit and Accountant	350	
Training	103	
PAYMENTS – CAPITAL		
Additions to Office Equipment	5,579	
		38,806
EXCESS OF PAYMENTS OVER RECEIPTS		9,666
OPENING BANK & CASH BALANCE		10,486
CLOSING BANK & CASH BALANCE		820
REDUCTION IN CASH BALANCE & BANK		9,666

This column is added and carried over.

Double lines means that this particular 'sum' is completed.

at the beginning of the year

at the end of the year

C.D.E.G. Limited

INCOME AND EXPENDITURE ACCOUNT
for the year ended 31st March 1986

		1986		1985
INCOME	£	£	£	£
Grants Receivable (see page 46)		28,000		32,945
Sundry Other Income and Fees		177		1,112
Bank Interest Received		963		183
TOTAL INCOME		29,140		34,240
LESS ADMINISTRATIVE EXPENSES				
Salaries – Gross (note 1)	23,755		13,789	
Subcontract Services	352		673	
Secretarial Services	823		–	
Rent, Rates and Insurances	1,029		404	
Fuel and 'Phone	1,399		1,058	
Postage, Stationery and Adverts	1,537		821	
Materials	157		25	
Subscriptions and Publications	384		22	
Transport	2,066		3,032	
Sundries	327		290	
Bank Charges	39		39	
Depreciation	900		61	
Audit and Accountant	250		437	
Repairs and Renewals	–		200	
Volunteers' Expenses	–		99	
Training	103		-	
		33,121		20,950
NET SURPLUS/(DEFICIT) FOR THE YEAR		(3,981)		13,290

These columns are totalled and then carried over to subtract in the next column.

Brackets is an accounting convention meaning *minus.*

Note 1: Salaries include £23,755 (1985 – £13,789) paid to members of the Management Committee.

These figures are based directly on the records of the organisation which relate to PAYMENTS and RECEIPTS (see preceeding page).

More commonly salaries are paid to paid workers who are not on the Management Committee but who are answerable to the Management Committee. Management Committee members are themselves very frequently unpaid. However, situations as the above *do* occur and should rightly be declared.

C.D.E.G. Limited

BALANCE SHEET
as at 31st March 1986

Usually items of plant & equipment.

	1986		1985	
	£	£	£	£
FIXED ASSETS (see page 50)		8,094		3,415
CURRENT ASSETS (due within 1 yr)				
Debtors and Prepayments	*84*		*136*	
Bank Balance	*1,739*		*11,176*	
Cash Balance	*10*		*3*	
	1,833		*11,315*	
CURRENT LIABILITIES (due within 1 yr)				
Sundry Creditors and Accruals	1,231		2,289	
Bank Overdraft	929		693	
	2,160		2,982	
NET CURRENT ASSETS/(LIABILITIES)		(327)		8,333
		7,767		11,748
Represented by:				
ACCUMULATED RESERVES BROUGHT FORWARD	11,748		(1,542)	
SURPLUS/DEFICIT FOR THE YEAR	(3,981)		13,290	
		7,767		11,748

ASSETS less LIABILITIES gives these figures

Money available from preceeding years.

This must be signed to be a valid set of accounts.

....

....

MEMBERS OF THE MANAGEMENT COMMITTEE

This explains how the Net Current Assets (Liabilities) have been arrived at.

This is the money in hand at the end of the year or, in some cases, the money that has been lost!

C.D.E.G. Limited

SCHEDULE OF FIXED ASSETS

		Office Equipment & Furniture
		£
Cost at 31st March 1985		3,654
Additions		5,579
		9,233
Depreciation 31 March 1985		239
Charge for the year		900
		1,139
Net Book Value at 31 March 1986		8,094
Net Book Value at 31 March 1985		3,415
Additions during the year are as follows:		
Slide Projector	27	
Filing Cabinet	115	
Desk and Chair	268	
Answerphone	40	
Photocopier	1,729	
Calculator	12	
Easel	187	
Video Recorder	550	
Video Player	546	
Kettles	26	
Word Processor	2,079	
	5,579	

Book value is the value of an organisation arrived at by the accountant and it may not have much relevance to actual value. For example, a vehicle may be depreciated over five years, this means that for a vehicle bought for £5000, £1000 will be 'written off' each year for five years at the end of which time the vehicle, as far as Book Value is concerned, will be worthless even if you could still sell it.

account. However, many items of expenditure or income are often combined in it, and so precise details of where the group's money came from and where it went cannot be distinguished. Additionally, the Income and Expenditure Account will leave out or add sums that may be owed to the group or by the group and which, therefore, do not appear as either receipts or payments. The absence from, addition to, or combination of, figures in the Income and Expenditure Account can be puzzling without a Receipts and Payments Account to refer to. The Receipts and Payments Account can be a very useful stepping-stone for helping interested parties within and outside your group to understand how the Income and Expenditure Account was arrived at.

Fourthly, you can add a sheet detailing just exactly what items of capital equipment are represented in the figures on the Balance Sheet. It is often very helpful to have a reminder of those items that were bought during the year because it gives greater meaning to what may sometimes seem a very large figure.

Finally, you need to remember that your final accounts play a very important part in representing your work. You will be sending them to other groups and bodies, perhaps as part of a request for funds, who may never come to meet you or see what you are doing. The final accounts of your group and the covering letter you send may be the only things available to the people who are deciding whether to approve your request for cash. The final accounts can act as a very important ambassador for your group and its work. It is therefore vital that the final accounts give the information you wish to put across and perform the function you wish them to perform. Your accountant is there to render you a service and you should feel confident about discussing with them exactly the service you require and ensuring that you receive it.

The Auditor

Throughout this book 'accounts' and 'accountant' and 'audit' and 'auditor' appear. They are not quite the same thing. It is worth discussing here exactly what an audit is and who performs one, and how they differ from an accountant.

The accountant writes up the accounts in the way shown in the model. The auditor is an independent and, properly, a third party who looks at these compiled accounts to ensure that the job has been done correctly. The accountant requires all the cheque stubs, invoices, scraps of receipts, as well as the files in which records have been kept in order to do their job. Ordinarily the auditor only requires the CASH OF BANK BOOK, the PETTY CASH record and the MINUTES of the Management Committee meetings.

It is the responsibility of auditors to report on any weaknesses in internal control which they have noted. Common examples of weakness are petty cash irregularities which result in the petty cash frequently being short because of open use by all members. Where internal control is especially weak they may also need to dig further and refer to all the back-up documents used in compiling the accounts. In general, however, when there is nothing wrong or out of the ordinary, the auditor's job is relatively straightforward and for most small voluntary organisations or other groups the same individual will perform the functions of both auditor and accountant.

7
If Things Go Wrong

This chapter is not just concerned with what to do when the time comes to pay the bills and there is no money in the account with which to pay them. Clearly that would be a case when things had gone wrong! When things get to such a pitch it is really a case of it being 'too late' for many of the techniques described in this book to help. If you follow the good practice suggested in this book, then, hopefully, such disasters can be averted before the situation becomes desperate. Nonetheless, sometimes things begin to go wrong in even the most carefully-run group. The systems suggested in this book are important precisely because the earliest indications of most common financial management problems are revealed through their use.

Within your Control?

First, it is important for you to ask if the problems lie within your control or outside it. If the petty cash never balances then that is within your control. If your group is concerned with supporting women who are victims of violence and the refuge burns to the ground and everyone needs temporary housing in bed and breakfast at £10 per person per night, then that is largely outside your control and it can only be hoped that you were carrying adequate insurance to cover such an eventuality.

Even if, as in the case of the burned refuge, your problems are caused by factors largely outside your control, then careful management systems may make them easier to cope with. The question of insurance is often never tackled in small organisations and yet inadequate cover can be literally devastating. Where financial management procedures include things like budgeting and careful record-keeping, questions of insurance can be resolved more easily than where no financial planning exists. This is because insurance is the sort of expense that budgeting should automatically ask questions about, such as, 'is it enough this year?' And good records will ensure an accurate assessment of costs and damage.

Another instance of circumstances outside your control may be the abolition of a funding body. This has recently been seen in the abolition of the Metropolitan County Councils. Certainly no voluntary organisation alone could have prevented these abolitions, but, they should, at least, have planned for the consequences of abolition. Of course, no-one is suggesting that unforeseen events can always be allowed for. But where management procedures are correct and financial planning is undertaken, the extent of disappointment or disaster caused by external factors can be proportionally diminished. Of course a burned refuge is bad news, of course the disappearance of a major funder is worrying, but it is far less bad and far less worrying if good accounting practice exists to help carry a group through.

Additionally, good accounting practice will inform a group faced with a crisis, almost immediately, just exactly what the extent of that crisis might be in financial terms. How many nights can we afford to keep our refuge residents in bed and breakfast, for example? How long can we continue to operate now that our funding from the County Council has come to an end?

Once those answers have been given, then a group can then reasonably ask 'what do we do next?' The accounts will show clearly what money is available to tackle the immediate problem; but what about the longer term? Well-kept records will form an impressive argument for further grants which may offset the immediate losses. They will be useful, too, if a short term overdraft is needed from the bank. They will indicate at a glance where priority spending has been over the past year and how the group itself can economise in order to continue the priority work: for example, reducing the 'phone bill by restricting all outgoing calls to after 1.00pm, funding staff tea and coffee by initiating a kitty, eliminating casual wages by deciding to perform certain tasks on a voluntary basis, lowering fuel bills by not heating the corridors, and so on. It is not uncommon for groups to decide to make savings and then choose the worst, least effective areas to make them in. Good accounts are an honest guide.

Management Procedures

Where circumstances seem to be within your control and yet your group is still having financial difficulties it is equally important to examine financial management procedures. One common source of financial problems is the system for dealing with PETTY CASH. Should one person be responsible for PETTY CASH or should all members have access to it? Every group must reconcile the disadvantages of having an open PETTY CASH system which may have frequent small discrepancies with the need to produce an accurate and faultless account of every detail of their financial activities to show their funding bodies or their accountant.

Another unwelcome financial problem, loss of cash, is most definitely within the control of a group. Minor discrepancies should be discovered regularly if the proper procedures for operating a petty cash system are adopted, and almost all groups are aware of the importance of monitoring petty cash even if many of them fail to do so. But often groups simply do not realise the implications of actually handling and storing larger amounts of cash. There will be a limit for which you are insured for having cash on the premises or for transporting cash to the bank. It is vital to be aware what these limits are and to work within them.

Ensuring that members of the management committee countersign invoices and cheques helps to keep the accountant happy and the records clear of any problems relating to misappropriated funds. Just as with a petty cash system, the spending of money needs to be approached with a degree of responsibility balanced by the need to get things done effectively and efficiently. This double signing technique avoids time and confusion later if any questions concerning payments occur.

Loss of control may also happen if a group has too many creditors. Unpaid bills mask the true state of the group's finances. There is a strong case for at least writing cheques promptly in payment of invoices, even if you do not send them immediately. This is because once a cheque has been written it will be registered in the BANK BOOK as an out-going amount. Therefore it will automatically be included in any actual figures compiled from the BANK BOOK.

All too often financial matters are kept in the hands of one or two people in an organisation with the result that others do not understand and cannot take responsibility for the group's financial situation. Commonly, groups try to overcome this by involving everyone in the mechanics of financial management, perhaps by rotating the responsibility among the members. This can also be a recipe for disaster, with no one individual having a clear picture of exactly what is happening. There is nothing wrong with only one or two people being responsible for keeping the records *provided that* the information they compile is open to everyone, and everyone is encouraged to understand the implications of it.

Regular meetings are vital to the smooth running of most organisations. Apart from keeping members communicating with each other, and the morale of the group high, they are essential for informing everyone concerned about the financial affairs of the group. Meetings are also usually the place to elicit some indication from the group as to what the next steps for the organisation should be once members have discussed the financial implications of any proposals that have been presented. Regular meetings of this kind equip members with the information to help them respond to events quickly and decisively. Over the months all members will build up a picture of how the group functions, so that if crises occur when something must be done, and done rapidly, everyone is ready to act.

It is important to remember that regular meetings will only be really useful if a careful record of decisions and of presented information is kept. All voluntary groups need to be thorough about writing down the minutes of their meetings so that they can be referred to for guidelines and information.

Help from Outside

Help from outside the group can take the form of advice or out-and-out rescue. Apart from the accountant, who is the obvious source of advice, other voluntary organisations or groups in your area may also be able to offer worthwhile comments on any difficulties that you have. They often have great sympathy with like-minded groups and, if they have been operating for a long time, a wealth of experience which they can share in a language which is often easier to understand than that of the professionals.

Equally, small local firms with a commitment to the area can be very supportive and again, like other voluntary groups, will often be able to explain things clearly because they, too, have had to learn from the beginning and will recognise your problems from their own experience. Community links are always to be encouraged for any group. It is surprising and gratifying how frequently other groups and small businesses, co-ops and commercial firms alike, will actively want to take part in your work.

There will always be the unfortunate groups that despite all good advice and care will disintegrate. This may be for reasons totally unconnected with the work of the group itself, for example, the disappearance of a major funding body, or perhaps because of personality problems which a group feels unable to overcome, or even because of the illness or death or resignation of one or several members. Coping with the end of a voluntary organisation is something in which the help of your accountant is vital, and they should be your first call. Some other helpful agencies are listed on page 00. Even when a group has to cease operating, you will still find that the financial records that have accumulated during its lifetime will be very helpful in making the close-down less painful. They will make it easier to complete the work of the group tidily, and to record for the members and perhaps even for other groups ways in which things were done well and ways in which things could have been improved.

8 Conclusion

Because voluntary organisations and other small groups are voluntary and often non-profit making, and therefore differ substantially from commercial organisations, it is possible to forget that they are nonetheless *organisations*. In order to function best, they need therefore to adopt organisational skills. The first step towards doing this is to understand that basic accounting procedures are simply techniques for organising information about money, and, as such, are powerful aids to effective organisation. Recording, analysing and reconciling have all featured in the preceding chapters. All can be adapted, to a greater or lesser extent, to the running of any group, provided that its members understand their value.

This is not to suggest that voluntary organisations or other groups become so bureaucratic that they lose their ability to respond flexibly to the circumstances around them. Rather, this book suggests that they consider how much better they could perform if the techniques of financial organisation employed by successful commercial firms were adapted to their own needs. Many of these financial techniques have been described in this book. They have been advocated as a means to help groups function more effectively, so that the vital work which they undertake, and upon which every person in Britain is in some way dependent, can expand and develop. There is no need for voluntary organisations either to be ashamed of the cash that they handle or to underestimate its importance. It is an essential tool which we need to know how to use effectively in order to improve the way in which we all live.

APPENDIX 1: COMMUNITY ACCOUNTING PROJECTS

Voluntary organisations frequently seek professional help from accountants. This can prove expensive, and, while many accountants offer their services free to voluntary groups, or charge only a nominal amount, this kind of free 'help' can have certain disadvantages. A non-paying organisation must sometimes come bottom of the list when it comes to an accountant's priorities. This is in no way to suggest that accountants lack commitment to helping voluntary bodies, but like everyone else, they do need to eat! Also, if you do not pay for a service, or pay very little for it, then it is hard to make demands upon the provider of that service. Voluntary organisations which receive free accounting help from an accountant in commercial practice can find it very difficult, if not impossible to criticise that accountant's work.

It is also unreasonable to expect a professional accountant to teach you how to do the job. Because accountants are frequently very busy they seldom have the time to show their clients how to either keep their accounts or to interpret them, and so voluntary organisations often find that they stumble on in the dark from year to year. And it is not their job to train others to become amateur accountants! In any case, if your finances are limited, full-scale professional help may be beyond your means. Since, as we have seen, it can be awkward to rely on free professional help, an alternative worth considering is to find your local Community Accounting Project or CAP.

Community Accounting Projects operate in various parts of the country. They have developed to meet the requirements of voluntary groups which have recognised that they have a need for accountancy support and have then organised a way of getting it for themselves. CAPs have two functions. Their first, and sadly most often used, function is that of 'rescue', coming in to help a voluntary organisation or other small group in crisis when things have got out of hand. Their second function is one of training, of trying to equip the members of voluntary organisations with the knowledge and understanding to look after their own money effectively. Existing CAPs offer a widely differing range of services but all have in common an aim to support voluntary organisations and community groups in the way in which these organisations wish to be supported.

The funding of CAPs often has a great affect on the type of support and services they are able to offer. Some are funded by the local authority, some by charitable trusts, some by Councils for Voluntary Service and some by combinations of these. A CAP that has the type of funding that frees them to choose to be accountable to their client group equally with, or in rare cases, over and above, their accountability to their funding body will, not surprisingly, have a greater flexibility to respond to clients' problems as and when they arrive than one which is 'tied' to guidelines imposed by its sponsors. As one CAP reports:

We began to work with the intention of solving crises as they arrived. But it soon became apparent that what was needed was the sort of training that would help to prevent these crises occurring in the first place. So we began a training programme which we run in several ways with the aim of de-mystifying the whole business of book-keeping, by helping groups to create simple accounting models. We always emphasise that the purpose of doing this is so that the management groups of voluntary organisations are themselves able to make informed decisions.

Another of our functions is to increase confidence among voluntary groups so that they feel they can tackle accounting in general, from simply keeping a decent, tidy set of books to the broader issues where, for example, members who have to fight for a grant will have all the accounting tools necessary to do so.

Finally we try to help groups to resolve the conflict which often exists between money being viewed as somewhat mucky and the ideals of the organisation which are often viewed as rising above financial considerations. We have found this conflict is a common plague of voluntary organisations and it lies at the root of many poor accounting procedures. Resolving this conflict often happens quite naturally as people learn about how to keep books and their confidence increases, nonetheless we try to stay aware of its possible existence and to help when asked.

This CAP is also interested in the way in which its members are committed to what they refer to as their 'social audit'. This means the way in which the CAP feels itself to be responsible to the groups that use it. It regularly asks itself and its client groups how well the CAP is serving the community and how far the activities of the CAP are contributing to local community consciousness. Through an examination of its work, the CAP evaluates how well it is helping voluntary groups achieve what they want to achieve. The CAP believes that this social audit is central to its continued success in doing what is useful for the community.

This CAP will help any group out in a crisis, but it sees its main role as one of training and support, as preventative rather than curative medicine, and it hopes that ultimately its services will become completely redundant. Apart from the flexibility to define its own role that this CAP enjoys, it is also able to employ several workers who can afford to spend time with clients in a way that some CAPs with fewer resources find very difficult.

In contrast, there are CAPs where only one community accountant is employed. In this type of CAP, the accountant is usually funded directly by the local authority and has to offer a wide range of services under the overall control of that authority. Although the funding comes from the same source as the first CAP discussed above, there the similarities end. The following case-study highlights some of the attendant problems:

A single accountant was employed by the local authority and was initially totally unsupported. Not only was he expected to undertake the varied and very demanding work of community accountant completely alone and without any back-up service but he also found himself responsible for certain aspects of insurance brokerage, transport and community photocopying! He was also responsible for all the funding: monitoring it and accounting for it. It is difficult to see how he could hope to be able to provide the comprehensive community accounting scheme that is presently available in other areas without a considerable change in policy.

To his great credit, this one-man CAP continued to try to provide some measure of training and support for at least newly-funded groups. Recently some of the original components of his job such as insurance and photocopying services have been cut back so that at last the accountant is able to concentrate more fully on the training needs of a wider range of groups. As the CAP reports:

The experience of this CAP has without doubt been a frustrating one. The long-term effects of the work of a community accountant in our area are difficult to predict with any positive surety when the responsibilities are so diverse, and when we are tied to funding rather than being independent of it and controlled by the groups we aim to serve.

There are other CAPs which have been initiated under the umbrella of local Councils for Voluntary Service (CVS). One set up to help local voluntary groups with their financial problems was originally funded under the Inner Area Programme and is now in a city council's main programme. Their financial advisor has described the workings of this CAP as follows:

In the first stages of the service most of the work was concerned with setting up book-keeping systems for new projects and assisting existing projects which were experiencing difficulties with their book-keeping.

We now provide voluntary groups with routine assistance with grant applications, advice for groups on financial policy, help with setting up book-keeping systems, training in basic accountancy such as wages and budgeting, and an emergency service for groups with financial and accounting crises.

We also oversee a book-keeping service that groups can buy. This service consists of professional book-keepers who will visit groups and keep their records for them. They charge a standard rate for the job but are monitored by the CVS Financial Adviser so that the client can be sure of getting value for money. This service often works out far more economically than employing a book-keeper on the staff of a voluntary organisation.

A further interesting scheme run by this CAP is their computerised wages service which any voluntary group can buy in to. Once an initial fee has been paid to set up a system for a group there is a nominal charge per pay slip. This service is also overseen by the Financial Adviser of the CVS and provides an inexpensive and efficient service.

Getting a CAP going

If your group could benefit from a CAP then it is worth finding out from your local CVS or local authority if such a facility exists in your area. If you find the information difficult to obtain, or conflicting, then the Urban Unit at the National Council for Voluntary Organisations, whose address is in appendix 4, will be able to help you further.

If you have no CAP in your area, then you can consider campaigning for one. You can begin by talking with other voluntary organisations in your area to see if they too are interested. Then take your ideas to a public forum and/or try to find an umbrella organisation that would be interested in housing the CAP. Either the local authority or the CVS are obvious possible choices. Then you need to co-ordinate applications for grants to fund the project and, where necessary, to lobby the council. It all sounds very easy on paper but it may well involve a lot of time and effort to establish a CAP. Nonetheless, now that successful projects exist it is far easier to convince local authorities and other funding bodies of the value and importance of CAPs, and you should proceed with a fair chance of success.

In conclusion, the still quite new and not very widespread experience of CAPs poses many questions and problems. Some of these, like the CAP where too much unrelated work was expected of a single person, may not be solved for some time. How far-reaching the training they provide will prove to be is impossible to foresee. Certainly, on present experience, they cope with a wide range of problems, some of which arise from the failure of voluntary groups themselves to understand money and some caused by the reactions of institutions even as large as the Manpower Services Commission, which fails to apply a standard for accounting procedures to all the groups who are responsible to it.

CAPs can sometimes help voluntary groups with other money matters. They may be able to assist groups to attract whatever funds they can. Above all, CAPs hope to lead groups to a clear understanding of what they wish to achieve in financial terms, to really see how money works and to teach an appreciation of financial management.

Voluntary organisations can help themselves and CAPs both by using CAP services and by applying basic financial 'good-housekeeping' skills. As a result CAPs will have fewer or even no financial crises to sort out. These are always time-consuming for CAPs and often very sad for everyone. CAPs will then be in a far better position to spend time on training and confidence-building.

APPENDIX 2: SOME ACCOUNTANCY TERMS

Capital Expenditure money spent on fixed assets.

Creditor someone to whom you owe money.

Debtor someone who owes you money.

Depreciation a way of accounting for the fact that fixed assets and capital assets will eventually wear out. In the most common sort of depreciation called 'straight line' depreciation, the value of item is divided by the number of years it is agreed it will last and then each year in the final accounts that amount is allowed against the income as an expense.

Fixed Assets those items that exist from year to year, like typewriters and desks, and which are used in generating income.

Reserves money, or sometimes the 'worth' of an organisation, which is carried forward from one year to the next and which existed within the group *before* the accounts were drawn up.

Revenue Expenditure money spent in the day to day running of an organisation such as cash for wages, stationery, tea etc.

FURTHER READING

Accounting for Voluntary Organisations
Brian Courtney, published by the Northern Ireland Council for Voluntary Action, 2 Annadale Avenue, Belfast BT7 3JH.

This book is divided into sections, each one dealing with different aspects of accounting practice. A book of 'how' to do it.

How to Manage Your Money, If You Have Any
Trefor Lloyd, Andreas Michaelides, Ann Lappin, published by the Community Accountancy Project in Hackney, Liberty Hall, 489 Kingsland Road, London E8 4AU.

An excellent, and humerous, explanation of both 'how' and 'why' to keep the books.

Getting Started at York Cycleworks
Hugh MacPherson, published by York Cycling Campaign, 16 Lawrence Street, York YO1 3BN.

On the face of it this may seem an unlikely publication to turn to. Nonetheless the section on finance is brief, to the point, well written, easy to understand, and very useful for any small group beginning to outline their financial pictures, not least because the original members of the organisation described had to learn most of it as they went along.

Starting a Voluntary Group: The Legal Choices
Sally Capper, published in 1986 by NCVO.

Tax Benefits for Charities
Home Office, Voluntary Services Unit.
Copies of this useful booklet can be ordered by telephoning 01-213 7262.

A guide to the various legal structures available to voluntary organisations at their formation.

HELPFUL ORGANISATIONS

Your Local Community Accounting Project and Council for Voluntary Service, if they exist. It is also useful to contact other local organisations to share experiences and skills.

National Council for Voluntary Organisations (NCVO)
26 Bedford Square
London WC1B 3HU

Charities Advisory Trust
Radius Works
Back Lane
Hampstead
London NW3 1HL

Charities Aid Foundation
48 Pembury Road
Tonbridge
Kent TN9 2JD

Co-operative Development Agency
Broadmead House
20 Albert Embankment
London SE1 7TJ

Industrial Common Ownership Movement (ICOM)
7–8 Corn Exchange Street
Leeds LS1 7BP

Charities Deposit Fund
77 London Wall
London EC2

OFFICIAL ACCOUNTING STANDARDS

Accounts prepared by professional accountants, that is by trained men and women who are members of one of the following bodies:

The Institute of Chartered Accountants in England and Wales
The Institute of Chartered Accountants of Scotland
The Institute of Chartered Accountants in Ireland
The Association of Certified Accountants
The Institute of Cost and Management Accountants
The Chartered Institute of Public Finance and Accountancy,

will be prepared according to certain nationally-agreed standards. These standards are normally referred to by their initials as SSAPs (Standard Statements of Accounting Practice) or SORPs (Statements of Recommended Practice). SSAPs are mandatory, but SORPs are only advisory. The requirements laid down by SSAPs and SORPs are complex and technical; it is not normally necessary for small groups to concern themselves with the details. Your professional advisor will tell you if your method of presenting your accounts does not comply with these legal requirements. Steps can then be taken to make your accounts acceptable.

There is, however, one new SORP in preparation which directly affects all those voluntary groups which are charities. Called 'Accounting by Charities', it aims to encourage good practice in financial record-keeping and money management. At present, its status is that of a consultative document (known as 'Exposure Draft 38'), but it should appear as a new SORP in 1987/88. Many voluntary groups will find it very helpful when they are trying to organise their finances. Copies may be obtained from the Accounting Standards Committee, The Institute of Chartered Accountants, P.O. Box 433, Moorgate Place, London EC2P 2BJ.